Oliver Optic

Snug Harbor

Or, The Champlain Mechanics

Oliver Optic

Snug Harbor
Or, The Champlain Mechanics

ISBN/EAN: 9783744797955

Printed in Europe, USA, Canada, Australia, Japan

Cover: Foto ©Andreas Hilbeck / pixelio.de

More available books at **www.hansebooks.com**

The Boat-Builder Series

SNUG HARBOR

OR

THE CHAMPLAIN MECHANICS

BY

OLIVER OPTIC

AUTHOR OF "YOUNG AMERICA ABROAD," "THE GREAT WESTERN SERIES," "THE ARMY AND NAVY SERIES," "THE WOODVILLE SERIES," "THE STARRY-FLAG SERIES," "THE BOAT-CLUB STORIES," "THE ONWARD AND UPWARD SERIES," "THE YACHT-CLUB SERIES," "THE LAKE-SHORE SERIES," "THE RIVERDALE STORIES," "ALL ADRIFT,"
ETC., ETC.

WITH ILLUSTRATIONS

BOSTON
LEE AND SHEPARD, PUBLISHERS
NEW YORK
CHARLES T. DILLINGHAM
1884

TO MY YOUNG FRIEND

HARRY CLINTON WHITE

This Book

IS AFFECTIONATELY DEDICATED.

PREFACE.

"SNUG HARBOR" is the second volume of "THE BOAT-BUILDER SERIES." Though it contains its fair proportion of story and adventure, there is less of these elements than in its predecessor; though the writer believes there is enough to keep up the interest of his young readers. Dory Dornwood, the hero of the initial volume of the series, is again presented, and about a quarter of a hundred others; though all of them cannot be heroes. Like the former volume, the scene is laid on Lake Champlain and its shores.

In accordance with the hint thrown out in the preface of the first volume, the Beech-Hill Industrial School makes a beginning in this book; and its pupils are gathered together in the schoolroom and the workshop. The boys are instructed only in those branches of learning which will be of the greatest practical utility to them as mechanics. They are taken into the shop, and set to work as carpenters and machinists; and some idea is given of their operations at the bench. But in a work of this kind the author finds it hardly practicable to describe in detail the work done by the Champlain mechanics; though he has done so to some extent, as a suggestion rather than as a system of instruction for boy-workmen. Without a vast number of drawings, the tools and machinery used by the carpenter and machinist cannot be described and explained so as to be of any great practical service. The book is rather to create an interest in these trades than to furnish a guide to young mechanics.

The author regrets that there is no American work of the kind mentioned. Our English cousins have sent us over some excellent works on the subject, which are very useful, though not fully adapted to the needs of American boys. A new friend suggests that such a book be prepared, and with his aid it may yet be done.

Captain Gildrock, the founder and patron of the Beech-Hill Industrial School, has some radical ideas on the subject of education; and probably many of the older readers of this book will disagree with him: but the question he argues is worthy of attention and discussion, however it may be finally settled.

Though the author is not a mechanic by trade, he has worked in his own shop for many years. With the carpenter's bench, the turning-lathe, and the various implements for working in wood and metals, he finds not only his needed exercise, but a degree of pleasure which makes it all the more healthy and exhilarating; and he commends the work to his young friends, both for their amusement and instruction.

DORCHESTER, MASS., Aug. 20, 1883.

CONTENTS.

CHAPTER I.
THE SLOOP THAT WENT TO THE BOTTOM . . . 13

CHAPTER II.
THE YOUNG MAN WITH A LONG NAME 23

CHAPTER III.
MR. BOLINGBROKE MILLWEED TELLS HIS STORY . . 34

CHAPTER IV.
THE GOLDWING ANCHORS FOR THE NIGHT . . . 44

CHAPTER V.
A QUARREL ON BOARD OF THE JUNIPER . . . 54

CHAPTER VI.
THE IMPULSIVE ASSAULT OF THE ENGINEER . . 65

CHAPTER VII.
BOLINGBROKE MILLWEED OUT OF A PLACE . . . 76

CHAPTER VIII.
PUPILS FOR THE BEECH-HILL INDUSTRIAL SCHOOL . 87

CHAPTER IX.
THE VOLUNTEER HELMSMAN AND HIS MOVEMENTS . 97

CONTENTS.

CHAPTER X.
The Battle near Garden Island 107

CHAPTER XI.
The Master-Carpenter disposes of his Prisoner, 117

CHAPTER XII.
Captain Gildrock's First Lesson in Navigation . 128

CHAPTER XIII.
Handling a Steamer in a Fog 138

CHAPTER XIV.
The Strong-Room at the Beech-Hill Industrial School 148

CHAPTER XV.
Something about the Affairs of the Millweed Family 159

CHAPTER XVI.
The Organization of the Ship's Company . . 170

CHAPTER XVII.
The Officers and Crew of the Sylph . . . 180

CHAPTER XVIII.
Another Battle at Plattsburg 190

CHAPTER XIX.
Something that happened on Shore . . . 201

CHAPTER XX.
The New Head of the Millweed Family . . 212

CONTENTS.

CHAPTER XXI.
PAGE
CAPTAIN GILDROCK ARGUES AGAINST HIGH-SCHOOLS, 223

CHAPTER XXII.
THE CHAMPLAIN MECHANICS IN THE SHOP . . . 234

CHAPTER XXIII.
SOMETHING ABOUT TOOLS AND WORK 244

CHAPTER XXIV.
WORK FOR THE HEAD AND THE HANDS . . . 255

CHAPTER XXV.
THE SECOND CLASS AT THE CARPENTER'S BENCH . 266

CHAPTER XXVI.
THE END OF THE FIRST SCHOOL-DAY AT BEECH HILL, 277

CHAPTER XXVII.
OSCAR CHESTER TAKES A LESSON IN BOATING . . 288

CHAPTER XXVIII.
THE UPSETTING OF THE MONKEY AND ITS LESSON . 299

CHAPTER XXIX.
AN AFTERNOON IN THE MACHINE-SHOP . . . 310

CHAPTER XXX.
WHAT THE STUDENTS FOUND AT THOMPSON'S POINT . 320

SNUG HARBOR;

OR,

THE CHAMPLAIN MECHANICS.

CHAPTER I.

THE SLOOP THAT WENT TO THE BOTTOM.

"STARBOARD your helm! hard a-starboard!" shouted Dory Dornwood, as he put the helm of the Goldwing to port in order to avoid a collision with a steam-launch which lay dead ahead of the schooner.

"Keep off! you will sink me!" cried a young man in a sloop-boat, which lay exactly in the course of the steam-launch.

"That's just what I mean to do, if you don't come about!" yelled the man at the wheel of the steamer. "Why didn't you stop when I called to you?"

"Keep off, or you will be into me!" screamed the skipper of the sloop, whose tones and manner indicated that he was very much terrified at the situation.

And he had reason enough to be alarmed. It was plain, from his management of his boat, that he was but an indifferent boatman; and probably he did not know what to do in the emergency. Dory had noticed the sloop coming up the lake with the steam-launch astern of her. The latter had run ahead of the sloop, and had come about, it now appeared, for the purpose of intercepting her.

When the skipper of the sloop realized the intention of the helmsman of the steamer, he put his helm to port; but he was too late. The sharp bow of the launch struck the frail craft amidships, and cut through her as though she had been made of card-board.

The sloop filled instantly; and, a moment later, the young man in her was struggling on the surface of the water. The boat was heavily ballasted, and she went down like a lump of lead. It was soon clear to Dory that the skipper could not swim, for he screamed as though the end of all things had come.

Very likely it would have been the end of all things to him, if Dory had not come about with the Goldwing, and stood over to the place where the young man was vainly beating the water with his feet and hands. With no great difficulty the skipper of the Goldwing, who was an aquatic bird of the first water, pulled in the victim of the catastrophe, in spite of the apparent efforts of the sufferer to prevent him from doing so.

It was a very warm day towards the end of August, and a bath in the cool waters of Lake Champlain was not the worst thing in the world to take. The victim of the collision was more scared than hurt; and he lay in the bottom of the yacht, puffing and blowing like a black bass just stolen from his native element. He did not seem to be able to speak, and Dory thought he was making a great fuss about a very small affair.

The Goldwing had been headed across the lake when her skipper picked up the victim; and, when he was safely on board, she continued on her course. Dory had come out to cool off and take a sail, and it made no difference to him where he went. The Beech-hill Industrial School had not yet commenced operations, and he had nothing on earth to do the greater part of the time.

His father had died a few weeks before; but he had found a snug harbor at Beech Hill, where he resided with his mother and sister in the elegant mansion of his uncle, Captain Royal Gildrock. The captain had acquired an immense fortune by his operations in various parts of the world; but as his wife was dead, and he had no children, it had bothered him a good deal to determine what to do with all his money.

For many years there had been a feud between the head of the Dornwood family and the owner of Beech Hill. Mr. Dornwood was an intemperate man, and never more than half supported his family; though he had good wages as a pilot on the lake. He had married the captain's only sister in spite of the opposition of all her friends, and especially of her brother.

When the captain attempted to assist his sister in taking care of her two children, her husband ordered him out of his house; for a great many sharp words had passed between them. The wife was afraid of her inebriate husband, and the attempts of the wealthy brother to help the family had ended in the complete estrangement of the brother and sister.

But as soon as Mrs. Dornwood was a widow, the captain hastened to her assistance. Though Dory had made an earnest effort to support the family, he had finally consented to reside with his mother at Beech Hill. The pilot's wife and children had always lived in the humblest tenements, worn the meanest garments, and lived upon the plainest and cheapest food.

Their lot at the new home was in tremendous contrast with their former condition. Captain Gildrock was a plain man himself, and inclined to regard the elegancies and luxuries of life with contempt. Though his house was large, it was plainly furnished. If his table was not garnished by the skill of a French cook, it was loaded with the best that could be procured. To the Dornwoods every thing about the house was luxurious.

Captain Gildrock was a thinking man, and he had ideas as well as money. The two go well together, for ideas are often barren things when one has not the means to carry them out. The worthy shipmaster had studied society and human nature in many lands and climes. After he retired from the sea and business generally, he had given his attention wholly to the affairs in his own country. After he had done so for a year or two, he was disposed to exclaim with the inspired writer, "Vanity of vanities! All is vanity!"

Perhaps the standard of the captain was too high for this world, but he felt that the American people were slipping away from first principles. The nation had prospered by toil, — by inducing and compelling the earth to yield her increase. Life had been something more than a pleasure-excursion.

"When I was young," he used to say, "the boys worked on the farm, learned a trade, or went to sea. Now all the young men go into stores, become counter-jumpers and man-milliners. Men get rich now by making corners, betting on futures, and in speculation of all sorts. A big thief is a gentleman : a little one is a criminal, after he is caught. The boys and girls have been educated too much : they get above their station in life, and then half starve themselves in order to be genteel."

The captain did not believe that the young people were educated too much; only that they were trained in useless accomplishments, as he regarded them. He did not think that the Genverres high-school, though a very successful institution in the opinion of the school-board and the citizens generally, was really a blessing to the town. He was confident that he had discovered the philosopher's stone in education, though he found himself almost alone in his opinions.

"That school only spoils good farmers and mechanics, good seamen and engineers. It gives them altogether too high notions of themselves. It turns its pupils out on the world fit only to be genteel. The education which the fathers of New England meant, when they planted the school-house alongside the church, was simply a common-school education, without any high-school bosh on the tail-end of it. It's all well enough for rich people: it is a luxury they can afford, and one they ought to pay for."

Very likely the captain was too ultra in his views, but the question he argued is one which must be settled before the lapse of many years.

The shipmaster was a practical man, and he did not talk without acting. He believed in industrial education, not in the grammar-school, but in place of the high-school. He had talked his views in town-meeting, and printed them in the papers; but the people were not inclined to adopt them.

A year before, he had taken a number of young men, and instructed them in seamanship and the construction and management of the marine engine. It was only a partial experiment, but he regarded it as an eminently successful one. Most of his pupils had obtained situations as engineers, and they were competent to fill them.

Captain Gildrock hoped to convince the people that his views were correct, and he was ready to spend his money in demonstrating the truth of what he preached. His class of the preceding year had been rather too old when he took them in hand. He wanted boys from the grammar-school, twelve or fourteen years old, before they had "bowed down to the vanity of this world," before they had learned to be genteel, before they oiled their hair, and spent half an hour a day in adjusting their neckties.

After the death of his brother-in-law, the pilot, he had captured his nephew, after a hard struggle, and found he was the leading spirit of the Goldwing Club, which had taken its name from Dory's boat. These boys were rather wild, but not bad. The captain succeeded in gathering them all into the Beech-hill Industrial School, as he decided to call the new institution. But the boys in Genverres were shy of the new school, or their parents were shy for them. Not a few of the latter regarded the retired shipmaster as a sort of harmless lunatic, liberal with his money, but, like all reformers, an unsafe leader to follow.

Several boys from the high-school had made excellent records out in the world, and each fond parent expected his own son would join the galaxy of bright stars from its graduates. The captain could find only three boys in the whole town who would join the new school, while thirty went to the high-school. Possibly the requirement that the pupils should reside at Beech Hill had some influence with the parents.

It looked as though the school was to begin with eight pupils, — hardly enough to man the Sylph, the captain's elegant steam-yacht, the largest and finest craft of the kind on the lake. All the boys in the high-school would have liked to flirt about the lake in the magnificent steamer;

but to do it as seamen, firemen, engineers, waiters, and cooks, was not wholly to the taste of the parents, if it suited that of the boys.

Dory Dornwood was waiting for the school to begin. Great boxes of tools, machinery, and other material for the workshops, had arrived at Beech Hill; but the captain would not allow them to be opened until the boys came. Besides, he was very busy in looking up pupils for the new institution. He wanted twenty-four to begin with, and he was searching for them in some of the interior towns where he was acquainted.

Dory was very impatient for the school to begin, though he was very happy in the midst of his new surroundings. He was a natural mechanic, and tools of any kind suited him better than books. He was fond of adventure, and wondered if he should ever have another time as lively as that on the lake before he was captured by his uncle.

The young man he had picked up on the lake was about sixteen years old, and was a stranger to him. His wet garments, though poor enough, betrayed an effort at some style. After a while he recovered his breath, and seemed to be in condition to give an account of himself.

CHAPTER II.

THE YOUNG MAN WITH A LONG NAME.

"YOU had a narrow squeak that time," said Dory Dornwood, as soon as he thought the victim of the disaster was in condition to do a little talking. "It is lucky you didn't get tangled up in the rigging of your boat. She went to the bottom like a pound of carpet-tacks; and she would have carried you down in a hurry if you hadn't let go in short metre."

"I think I am remarkably fortunate in being among the living at this moment," replied the stranger, looking out over the stern of the Goldwing. "That was the most atrocious thing a fellow ever did."

"What was?" inquired Dory, who was not quite sure what the victim meant by the remark, or whether he alluded to him or to the man in the steam-launch.

"Why, running into me like that," protested the passenger with no little indignation in his tones.

"Let me see, 'atrocious' means something bad or wicked, don't it?" continued Dory.

"Something very bad and very wicked," replied the stranger, with a sickly smile, as he bestowed a patronizing glance upon his deliverer.

"I thought it was something of that sort. I suppose you don't use such big words as that before breakfast, do you?"

"Why not before breakfast as well as after? It is a common word, in use every day in the week."

"I didn't know but it might put your jaws out of joint, and spoil your appetite," added Dory, as he glanced behind him to see what had become of the steam-launch.

"My appetite is not so easily spoiled."

"I suppose you came up from Burlington?" said Dory suggestively, as though he considered an explanation on the part of the stranger to be in order at the present time.

"I have just come from Burlington," answered the victim, who appeared to be disposed to say nothing more. "Do you suppose I can get that boat again?"

"I should say that the chance of getting her

again was not first-rate. She went down where the water is about two hundred and fifty feet deep; and it won't be an easy thing to get hold of her," replied Dory. "If you had let him run into you between Diamond Island and Porter's Bay, where the water is not more than fifty or sixty feet deep, you could have raised her without much difficulty. I don't believe you will ever see her again."

"That's bad," mused the stranger. "She did not belong to me."

"Then you are so much in. Perhaps, if she had belonged to you, you would not have let the steam-launch run into you," added Dory, who did not quite like the way the victim was taking things; for he did not seem to remember that he had been pulled out of the water by the skipper of the Goldwing when he was in great danger of drowning.

"I did not let the steam-launch run into me. The man in her did it on purpose. It was not an accident," answered the stranger.

"I heard the fellow say that he meant to sink you; and, after he said that, I thought you were a little out of your head to let him do it."

"I didn't let him do it."

"I thought you did. If I had been at the tiller of that sloop, he wouldn't have done it."

"Probably you are a better boatman than I am: I don't pretend to know much about the management of a yacht," replied the victim meekly, as he finished wiping the water from his face.

"Then you ought not to be sailing a boat in a fresh breeze, such as we are having to-day. Why didn't you put your helm down when you saw that he was going to run into you?"

"Down where?" asked the victim with a vacant stare.

"Down cellar!" exclaimed Dory, disgusted at the ignorance of the skipper of the sunken sloop. "No fellow ought to sail a boat if he don't know how to put the helm down."

"A fellow can't know every thing in the world."

"Then, I suppose you know every thing else: but how to put the helm down was the one thing you ought to have known, when that fellow was kind enough to tell you beforehand that he meant to sink you."

"Don't be too rough on me, Mr. — I don't know your name. I am under very great obligations to you for the signal service you have rendered me, and I shall be glad to know you better."

"My name is Theodore Dornwood,—Dory for short. What is yours?"

"Dory Dornwood!" exclaimed the victim, bestowing a look of astonishment upon the modest skipper. "I have heard of you before, and I am particularly glad to meet you."

"I should think you might be, since I picked you up in deep water. But you did not give me your name."

"My name is Bolingbroke Millweed."

"Is that all the name you have?" asked Dory, as he opened his eyes till they were as big as a pair of saucers — very small saucers. "I didn't quite make it out, for it fairly snarled up my intellect."

"Bolingbroke Millweed," repeated the stranger with a slight frown upon his brow. "It's all the name I have."

"It's name enough, I should say."

"It is hardly worth while to make fun of my name: I am not responsible for it, and it is the best I have."

"I beg your pardon, Mr. — I don't know what your name is now, for really I did not take it in," pleaded Dory, who was sometimes very brusk in his manner, though he did not mean to hurt anybody's feelings. "Honestly, I did not understand you."

"You cannot have read English history very much, or you would have recognized the first name."

"I never did read English history much: in fact, I never did much reading of any kind."

"My first name is Bolingbroke, and my surname is Millweed. The whole of it is Bolingbroke Millweed," added the victim, mollified as he pitied the ignorance of his deliverer.

"All right, Mr. Millweed: I won't tackle the first name until I get a little better acquainted with it."

"Viscount Henry St. John Bolingbroke, after whom I was named, was a prime minister of England, and a fine scholar; though he was charged with treason. But I did not pick out the name myself: it was my mother's choice, but I can't say that I approve it. I suppose I shall be called 'Bolly' as long as I live."

"Of course your friends can't handle such a jaw-breaker as Bolingbroke every time they want to ask you which way the wind is. But never mind the name, Mr. Millweed. I picked you up in deep water, and that's how you happen to be on board of the Goldwing."

"The famous Goldwing! I am extremely happy to be on board of her; though I wish our meeting had been under more favorable circumstances," added Mr. Bolingbroke Millweed, as he poured the water out of one of his shoes.

"I only said that you were on board of the Goldwing; and the question now is, what shall I do with you, for I see the steam-launch is headed this way. I should judge from his actions that the man at the wheel of her wants to see you."

"He does want to see me! I am the victim of a conspiracy!" exclaimed Mr. Millweed in tragic tones, as he sprang to his feet.

"The victim of a conspiracy? Is that what you call the sinking of a sloop?"

"I feel that the brave and noble Dory Dornwood will be my friend, and " —

"Clap a stopper on your jaw-tackle!" interposed the skipper of the Goldwing, borrowing an expression his uncle had quoted in his presence. "If you mean to blarney me, I shall be your enemy; and I will put you ashore on Diamond Island, without benefit of clergy."

"Excuse me: I did not mean to offend you, Mr. Dornwood,"—

"Avast heaving! Don't 'mister' me. Call me Dory; but don't call me too late for dinner," laughed the skipper.

"Since I know who you are, I shall tell you my story, and explain how I happened to be sailing the sloop, and "—

"I know how you were sailing her, and you sailed her to the bottom. Tell me the rest of it."

"I will tell you why that man ran into me, and why he was chasing me up the lake."

"That's the point; but make the yarn a short one, or the steam-launch will be upon us before you get through with it. You have the floor, Mr. Millweed," replied Dory, as he glanced at the approaching steamer.

"But I don't want to be caught by that man! It might be fatal to me. He is a conspirator; and he is seeking to destroy my good name," pleaded Mr. Millweed earnestly.

"I don't understand the matter. Is the man an officer?"

"Not at all: he is chief clerk in a store in Burlington, and the steam-launch belongs to his employer. But he is rapidly overtaking us," said the passenger.

"Why should he be after you? What have you been doing that is wrong?" asked Dory, who had no idea of enlisting on the wrong side in anybody's cause.

"I have done nothing wrong. I will tell you all about the matter, only don't let that man get hold of me. Upon my sacred honor, I am guilty of no crime," continued Bolingbroke Millweed.

Dory was greatly tempted. He had a reputation on Lake Champlain, won but a short time before he made his snug harbor at Beech Hill. On two occasions he had successfully kept out of the way of a steamer. He had been pursued all one day by the swiftest steam-yacht on the lake, but by his "tactics" he had kept out of her reach.

If the young man had been guilty of a crime,

he would do nothing for him. His passenger spoke fairly; but, if he had been doing wrong, he would not scruple to lie about it. Dory decided to keep out of the way of the steam-launch long enough to hear Bolingbroke's story. It was an exciting game to dodge a steamer, and he desired to play it. The water in the lake had been very low all summer, and no heavy rains had yet raised it. The low-water soundings on the chart needed no corrections.

The Goldwing was a schooner, and Dory had been sailing under jib and mainsail only. This was about all the sail she could comfortably carry. The skipper looked over the situation very carefully. The yacht was on the wind, headed across the lake. After the sinking of the sloop, the two men in the steamer had a long talk before they started her screw again; and she was all of half a mile astern of the Goldwing.

Coming up into the wind, Dory set the mainsail; and then it was a staggering wind for the Goldwing. By a little manœuvring the skipper brought Diamond Island between his own craft and the steam-launch.

The pursuer had gained on him while he was

THE YOUNG MAN WITH A LONG NAME. 33

setting the foresail. Starting his sheets, he stood off to the south-west until the steamer was abreast of the island. She could not head him off; and then he came about again, steering her due south.

The skipper was ready for the explanation, and the passenger proceeded to relate it.

CHAPTER III.

MR. BOLINGBROKE MILLWEED TELLS HIS STORY.

THE wind was blowing very fresh; and the Goldwing staggered wildly, as she went ahead nearly before it. Mr. Bolingbroke Millweed appeared to be a little nervous, for the schooner carried twice as much sail in proportion to her size as the sloop in which he had come from Burlington.

"She acts just as though she was going to tip over," said he, clinging to the wash-board.

"Tip over! She don't do that sort of thing. She has got over all her bad habits," replied the skipper. "But I should like to have you spin your yarn before we get up to Field's Bay, so that I may know what to do with you."

"I have been looking for a place in a store for a year, for I was graduated at the high-school last summer," Mr. Millweed began. "I know a young man by the name of Hackett Tungwood, who is in a store in Burlington. He wanted a vacation of a week, and he engaged me to take his place while he was absent."

"Did his boss agree to it?" asked Dory.

"His employer did agree to it, and treated me very kindly when I went to the store at seven o'clock this morning. About nine o'clock Mr. Lingerwell, who is Hack's brother-in-law, and the head man in the store, sent me to the safe for the cash-book."

"I got the book, and gave it to him. Just then Mr. Longbrook, the proprietor, came in, and asked Mr. Lingerwell for the four hundred and fifty dollars which had been put in the safe the night before. I saw the head man go to the safe, and then both he and his employer seemed to be in great consternation."

"Short words, or you never will finish," interposed Dory.

"I did not know what the matter was, but Mr. Lingerwell used a great many exclamations."

"What did he do with them?"

"He uttered them, of course: what else could he do with them? If you continue to interrupt with irrelevant questions, it will take me a long time to tell the story," replied Mr. Millweed impatiently. "I was putting up goods near the desk, or I should not have noticed what was going on. In a little while I heard enough to satisfy me that the four hundred and fifty dollars was missing.

"Mr. Longbrook called me to the desk, and asked if I had been to the safe. I told him I had taken the cash-book from the safe, as I had been told to do. He looked me sharply in the eye. Mr. Lingerwell said no one else had been to the safe since he opened it in the morning.

"I was sent back to my work, and the two men kept on talking about the money. It was clear enough to me that I was suspected of taking it, and I felt as though I was already in the State prison. I heard Mr. Lingerwell say he was sure I had taken the money, for it was all right when he opened the safe. I never was so terrified before in my life. Hack Tungwell had told me he did not expect to keep his place much longer: he might not return at all. If I pleased his employer, I might get the situation.

"What I heard seemed to be the knell of all my hopes. I had done my best to get a place, for my father sadly needs what little I could earn. Then the two men talked in low tones for a while.

Presently Mr. Longbrook went out of the store. I was sure he had gone for an officer to arrest me.

"The idea of being arrested and marched through the streets by a constable was about as bad to me as being shot through the head. When Mr. Lingerwell went to the back part of the store, I rushed out at the front door."

"You left!" exclaimed Dory with something like indignation in his tones.

"I did: I was wholly unwilling to be dragged through the streets by an officer."

"That was worse than sinking the sloop in two hundred and fifty feet of water. Do I understand you to say that you did not take the money from the safe?" demanded Dory.

"Do I look like a thief?" asked Mr. Millweed, rising from his seat in the standing-room in deep disgust; though he was immediately thrown back again by the motion of the yacht.

"Never mind how you look: you acted just like a thief," retorted Dory warmly. "You don't say yet that you didn't take the money when you went to the safe for the book."

"I do say now, most emphatically, that I did

not take the money when I went to the safe for the cash-book, or at any other time. I didn't even know there was any money in the safe," protested Mr. Millweed very earnestly.

"That's coming to the point; but you have done the best you could to convince your employer and his head man that you did take it. I advise you to go straight back to Burlington, and then straight to the store, and face the music. If anybody says I stole any money, I want to see the man that says so."

"That would all be very well under ordinary circumstances," pleaded Mr. Millweed.

"It's all very well under any circumstances."

"I had a theory of my own."

"I don't care any thing about your theory: I say the way is to face the music. If you had let them search you before you went out of the store, you would have been all right. They would not have found the money upon you, and you had had no chance to get rid of it. Now they will say you buried it somewhere on the shore of the lake."

"But I tell you I have a theory. I believe Tim Lingerwell took the money himself. How easy it would have been for him to slip the wallet, or the package, whatever it was, into my pocket when I was not looking."

"That thing has been done in a hundred and fifty novels and stories, but it isn't done every day in Burlington. If Tim Lingerwell wanted the money bad enough to steal it, he wouldn't put it into your pocket."

"He isn't any too good to do such a thing. He and Hack belong in Genverres; and people here wouldn't trust either of them with a pewter quarter," argued Mr. Millweed.

"Perhaps you are right: I don't know. You have given yourself away, and made it look bad for you. If Tim Lingerwell took the money, what did he do with it?"

"That's more than I know. He has the care of the safe, and he and I were the only persons who had been near it when Mr. Longbrook came in for the money. I know I did not take it; and if I didn't, he did. That's the whole of it."

Dory believed his passenger had been a fool to run away; but, without knowing why, he could not help believing that he was telling the truth.

"Where did you get the sloop in which you

came up the lake?" he asked. "You said she did not belong to you."

"She belongs to Sim Green, a friend of mine, who lives next door to me. He was going down to Burlington to stay a few days with his uncle. Money is a scarce article in our family, and I had none to pay my fare by railroad. I was going to walk; but, at Sim's invitation, I went down in his sloop. When I left the store, I went down to the boat, and got into it. Then I thought I would go home, and tell my father and mother what had happened."

"Then you took the boat without leave?"

"I knew Sim would not care, and he won't come home before Saturday. I meant to send it back before that time," Mr. Millweed explained.

"That may be all right; but Sim won't thank you for taking it, when he learns that she has gone down in two hundred and fifty feet of water. Now, what is to be done?" asked Dory. "Will you go back to Burlington, and face the music?"

"I don't know what to do," replied Mr. Millweed, evidently overwhelmed with perplexity.

"I have told you what I would do if I were in your place," added Dory.

"Then I will go back; but I don't want to be dragged into Burlington by Tim Lingerwell," replied Mr. Millweed, as he glanced at the steam-launch.

"All right, if you will only go back. What makes you think Tim Lingerwell took the money?" asked Dory.

"The more I think of it, the more certain I feel that he took the money. Why should he call me from my work to get the cash-book out of the safe for him, when he was within six feet of it? Why should he send me to the safe at all, and leave it unlocked, when he knew there was so much money in it? Why didn't he search me before Mr. Longbrook went out? He managed it all to suit himself," replied the passenger with energy.

Dory thought his passenger was right. If the head man in the store believed the substitute clerk had taken the money from the safe, he could not see why he had been permitted to leave the store.

"Did they chase you in the street after you left the store?" asked Dory, who was rather inclined to do a little detective business on his own account, as he had had a taste of it during the summer.

"No one chased me. I did not see any one from the store. I was off Split Rock when I first saw the launch, but I didn't know Tim was in her till just before he ran into the sloop. The moment I heard his voice, I understood it all; but I did not know enough about a boat to get out of the way."

"I don't believe you did, or you would not have sunk that sloop. The wonder is, that you got as far as you did without capsizing her."

"I hoisted the sail, and let her go. The wind was fair, and all I had to do was to keep her away from the shore. She frightened me out of my wits two or three times when the waves were high."

"With this breeze we can run away from that steam-launch. If you like, I will take you back to Burlington, after I have told my mother where I am going."

"I should like that very much," replied Mr. Millweed.

"But we can't run away from the steamer beating down the lake, and we must dodge her in some way," suggested Dory.

"I will do just as you say, Dory; and I begin to see what an idiot I was to run away, though I still think Tim Lingerwell had some plan to trip me up," added the passenger.

Dory had already decided upon his plan of operations. The steamer was on the wrong side of him: he wished he was below instead of above her; for he wanted to run into Beaver River, which he could not do on the open lake without encountering his pursuer.

His southerly course had by this time brought him near the east shore of the lake. The steam-launch was all of half a mile distant. From the mouth of the river a shoal extends a mile out into the lake, and over a mile to the southward. Dory struck this shallow water at its southern extremity.

The deepest water is near the shore, and the skipper followed it. The launch continued on her former course for a while, and then stopped her screw. Tim Lingerwell at the wheel was perplexed; but Dory found his way across the shoal, and entered the river. Then the launch went around the shoal, and continued the chase.

CHAPTER IV.

THE GOLDWING ANCHORS FOR THE NIGHT.

AS soon as the Goldwing was fairly in the river, Dory found the wind was light compared with what it had been on the open lake. But the skipper had made up his mind that his passenger should not be taken out of the boat: his plan for another movement was ready.

"She is catching us, and I might as well make up my mind to go back to Burlington in the Juniper;" for that was the name of the steam-launch. "I believe Tim Lingerwell has that money in his pocket at this minute; for he probably has had no chance to get rid of it," said Mr. Millweed in utter despondency.

"You can make up your mind any way you please; but, if you don't want to go with him, you needn't. If you will do as I say, I will land you in Burlington to-night," replied Dory, as the yacht passed the narrow neck of land between the river and Porter's Bay.

"I will do just as you tell me, Dory; for I know you are capable of doing big things."

"It won't be a very big thing, but we can dodge the Juniper a great deal easier than you can go to bed without your supper. I shall make a landing at the cross-cut. You will go on shore, and follow the path until you get to the other side of the woods. Then take the other path to the river, and strike it half a mile above the landing."

"What is all that for?" asked Mr. Millweed, perplexed by the instructions.

"You do just as I tell you, and ask no questions. I will be responsible for the result."

"All right: I will do so. But I might as well go home, for I shall be half-way there when I get to the other side of the woods."

"If you go home, Tim Lingerwell will find you there. He will think you have gone home; and that is just what I want him to think," said Dory, as he made the landing at the cross-cut, which was a short way to reach the northern outskirts of the town.

"I will do just what you say, Dory."

"Very well; but don't be in a hurry. Wait till the Juniper gets a little nearer, so that Tim can see you. Then start off as though you meant business."

They had not long to wait, for the steam-launch had been gaining rapidly on the yacht since they entered the river. When she was near enough to enable those on board of her to see just what was done, Mr. Millweed leaped ashore, and ran with all his might.

"Stop him! Don't let him go!" shouted the helmsman of the Juniper. "He is a thief! He has been stealing a large sum of money!"

"I am not a constable," answered Dory quietly. "I pulled him out of deep water, and brought him ashore. If you want him, you can take him."

Tim Lingerwell rang his bell, and the engine stopped. He ran her up to the shore, carrying her bow line to a post, as he leaped upon the bank.

"What did you let him go for?" demanded Tim, turning to Dory, who had also landed.

"It's none of my business where he goes," replied Dory. "This is a free country."

"But I told you he had been stealing. Come, Greeze, we must catch him. He lives up this way; and we shall find him at home, if we don't catch him before he gets there."

The engineer abandoned his machine, and the two men started off on a run in the direction taken by the fugitive. But Mr. Millweed had a good start, and the wood concealed him from his pursuers.

As soon as they were out of sight, Dory took a survey of the Juniper. He had often seen her before, though he had never been on board of her; and he improved the present opportunity to do so. He made a more careful examination of her than a mere inspection seemed to require. Like Mr. Millweed, he had a theory. He looked into all the lockers, and even examined the space under the ceiling as far as he could get at it.

Just as he was beginning to think his theory was entirely at fault, he drew out a large pocket-book, which seemed to be well filled with something. He opened it, and found that it contained a large pile of bank-bills. Mr. Millweed's theory was correct: Tim Lingerwell had had no opportunity to dispose of the money, and he had put it where he supposed no mortal could possibly find it.

Mr. Bolingbroke Millweed's honesty was demonstrated. Dory had been right in trusting him. It was a great satisfaction to him to find that he had judged his passenger correctly. But Tim Lingerwell was quite as big a fool as Mr. Millweed; and the same might be truly said of any person who commits a robbery.

Dory took the money from the pocket-book, and put it into his hip-pocket. He put a portion of a newspaper into the place from which he had taken the bills, so as to make the pocket-book look as it had before its valuable contents had been removed. Then he placed it under the ceiling precisely as he had found it. His business on board of the Juniper was finished, and he hastened to get the Goldwing under way again.

Mr. Millweed had faithfully followed his instructions, and was on the bank of the river above the woods. The passenger leaped on board when the bow touched the shore.

"Did you see them, Dory?" asked Mr. Millweed, greatly excited.

"Of course I saw them. They landed where you did, and started off at a dead run after you. Lingerwell said you had gone home; and they expect to find you there," replied Dory, as he headed the yacht on her course up the river again.

"They won't find me there," added the passenger, chuckling at the success of Dory's plan. "But won't they find us at Beech Hill if you go there?"

"It will be two hours before they get back to the Juniper again, and then they won't know where to look for you. We are all right."

Dory did not go into Beech-Hill Creek, which led to the lake in the rear of the mansion of Captain Gildrock, but continued on his course till he came to the river-road, on which the estate was located. At this point he made a landing; and, leaving his charge in the boat, he hastened to the house.

Dory found his mother and sister in the garden. As briefly as he could, he told the story of his passenger, and announced his intention of going to Burlington at once. As he did so, they walked to the house, where Mrs. Dornwood put up a heavy lunch for her son. The skipper showed the money he had taken from the Juniper, to prove his statement; but this was a secret she was not to reveal to any person at present.

Mrs. Dornwood volunteered to call upon the Millweeds, and inform them of the true state of the case; for the visit of Tim Lingerwell was likely to give them much trouble and anxiety before the whole truth came out.

With the large lunch-basket and his overcoat, Dory hastened back to the place where he had left the Goldwing. He found his passenger in a very nervous and troubled frame of mind, fearful that Tim Lingerwell might pounce upon him while he was waiting for the skipper. He re-assured him by his confident words, and they embarked without losing a moment.

"It is a little more than an hour since we left the steamer; and Lingerwell may see us as we go down the river, though I don't think he has got back yet," said Dory, when the yacht was under way.

"Why not wait here until after the Juniper has started?" suggested Mr. Millweed.

"We should have to wait all night, I think; for I don't believe Lingerwell will go back without you," replied Dory.

"But you have to sail back to Burlington with the wind against you: the Juniper will be sure to catch us," added Mr. Millweed anxiously.

"I am willing to take the chances; and, whatever happens to us, I will promise that you shall be all right when you have faced the music," answered Dory, keeping a sharp lookout ahead for the steam-launch.

"All right: you have carried me through so far, and I will trust you to the end. You saved my life; and I shall never cease to be grateful to you, even if you do nothing more for me," said the passenger with more feeling than he had before exhibited.

As the yacht approached the place where the fugitive had landed, Dory saw that the Juniper was still there. As the skipper was obliged to beat a portion of the distance down the river, he made a tack within twenty feet of her.

"Hold on, there!" shouted a voice from her; but it was not that of Lingerwell.

At the same moment a man rose from the bottom of the launch. He proved to be Greeze, the engineer. The pilot had evidently sent him back to attend to the boat.

"We will see you in Burlington," replied Dory, with abundant good nature, when he was satisfied that Lingerwell was not on board of her.

"We want that thief!" yelled Greeze.

"You will take him down to Burlington with you when you go."

Doubtless this answer perplexed the engineer; but the yacht passed out of hailing-distance, and no explanation was practicable. After going around the bend of the river, the Goldwing could lay her course for the lake, close-hauled.

"The engineer has left the boat again," said Mr. Millweed, just before the yacht reached the bend. "Where do you suppose he is going now?"

"He is going to find Lingerwell, and tell him that you have gone down the river. But he may not find him for two hours. Of course he is moving about looking for you. Very likely he will go to my uncle's house to inquire for me, though he will not be any the wiser for his visit. But I feel as though it was about supper-time," continued Dory, as he consulted the watch his uncle had given him on his last birthday. "It is quarter-past six."

"I have the same sort of a feeling; for I had no dinner to-day, and took my breakfast at six this morning," added Mr. Millweed.

"Why didn't you say so before? You might have been working your jaws from the time we left the shore-road," said Dory, as he handed the lunch-basket to his passenger. "Help yourself, and I will feed as the helm gives me time."

Mr. Millweed showed that he had an appetite by the time the Goldwing reached the lake. As the sun went down, the wind died out, though not till the schooner had passed Split Rock.

"I am afraid we shall not get to Burlington to-night; for we can't go without wind," said Dory, when the breeze had nearly deserted them.

"Then I am sure to be caught," added the passenger.

"Not at all: don't give it up."

Dory kept the boat moving a mile farther; and then came to anchor inside of Cedar Island, where the masts of the Goldwing could not be seen from the lake. At the skipper's suggestion, the passenger turned in, and went to sleep.

CHAPTER V.

A QUARREL ON BOARD OF THE JUNIPER.

DORY had put on his overcoat, and gone to sleep on the cushions of the standing-room. The jib had been lowered, but the fore and main sails were still set. The skipper had passed the main-sheet around his arm, so that any motion of the sail would wake him. This signal disturbed him about eleven by jerking him off the seat upon the floor of the standing-room.

The wind had begun to come in fresh between Garden Island and Thompson's Point, indicating that its direction was from the south-west. It was fair for Burlington; but, before he got up the anchor, he listened attentively for any sounds that might come from the open lake, for he had a suspicion that he heard something.

A moment later he was confident that he heard the puff of steam from the escape-pipe of a steamer. It was cloudy, and the night was dark. He looked out between the islands and the mainland, but he could see nothing. The sounds came nearer for a time: then they ceased for a few minutes, and were followed by a splash in the water. He was satisfied that a steamer had anchored at no great distance from Cedar Island.

The skipper's nap had refreshed him, and he was not inclined to sleep while there was wind enough to move the schooner. Very likely the steamer which had anchored was the Juniper. Probably Tim Lingerwell realized that the Goldwing could not sail without wind; and he was afraid he might pass her if he continued on his course. Doubtless he suspected that she had put in behind some island.

Dory got up the anchor, hoisted the jib, and, with the wind on the beam, stood off to the northwest. He had no doubt the steamer he had heard was the Juniper. The noise of her screw, and the puff of her escape-pipe, indicated that she was a very small craft. He concluded that Tim Lingerwell would keep a sharp lookout for him, and he expected to be chased as soon as he passed the island.

When he could see between the two islands, he discovered a light, which marked the position of the Juniper. The Goldwing passed within a quarter of a mile of her; but the wind was coming quite fresh from the south-west, and Dory thought that he could take care of himself and his sleeping passenger.

Though it was very dark, the skipper had not deemed it prudent to light one of his lanterns; for it would be sure to betray his presence. As the yacht continued silently on her course, Dory heard the sound of voices in the direction of Garden Island, behind which he could see the Juniper's light.

It was evident that the pursuers were not asleep. Dory listened with all his might, for he was deeply interested in what was taking place on board of the steam-launch. It seemed to him that the captain and engineer were talking a great deal louder than the occasion required. As they were in the same craft, it was hardly necessary for them to yell at each other. After he had listened a while, Dory thought the tones of the speakers were angry and even violent.

The skipper brought the Goldwing up into the wind, for a short distance farther would carry the yacht out of sight of the Juniper. He listened

A QUARREL ON BOARD OF THE JUNIPER. 57

again; and the tones of the crew of the steam-launch were more violent than before. What was the matter? There was clearly a quarrel in progress between the captain and the engineer. As the voices became louder and more forcible, the disputants were plainly approaching a crisis in the quarrel.

"Help! Help! Murder!" yelled one of the angry men; and Dory was confident it was the voice of the engineer.

The skipper of the Goldwing did not wait to hear any more, or to speculate upon the cause of the difficulty on board of the Juniper. Hauling in his sheets, he filled away on the starboard tack. The schooner could just lay her course for the steamer's light. It looked a little like a stormy time ahead, and Dory decided to call his passenger.

Leaving the helm for a moment, he went to the cabin forward; and a sharp word roused Mr. Millweed from his slumbers. Hastening back to the helm, he seized the tiller before the schooner had time to broach-to. At that moment the cry from the steamer was repeated, though it was fainter than before.

"What's the matter, Dory?" asked Mr. Millweed, as he rushed into the standing-room. "Didn't I hear a yell just now?"

"If you are not deaf, you did," replied Dory, still gazing at the steamer's light. "There is a row on board of the Juniper. The engineer is shouting for help."

"What does it all mean?" inquired the passenger anxiously.

"I don't know what it means, but I am going up there to find out."

"Do you think it is safe to go near them?" inquired Mr. Millweed.

"I don't know whether it is safe or not; but men don't yell murder in the middle of the night without some good reason."

"What can be the meaning of it?" asked the fugitive, evidently believing that the skipper ought to be able to tell him all about it.

"You can guess as well as I can, Bolly," answered Dory. "Tim and the engineer are the only persons on board of the Juniper, and the quarrel must be between them. That's all I know about it. But, if we are going to take a hand in this fight, we had better have some sort of weapons."

"You don't mean to take a hand in any fight, do you, Dory?" asked Bolingbroke, not a little alarmed at the announcement.

"Not if I can help it; but I don't mean to let Lingerwell kill his companion, without putting a finger in the pie. Go to the cabin, and bring out the long tiller. You will find it under the berth you slept in."

"But I don't like the idea of getting into a fight with such a fellow as Tim Lingerwell," protested Bolingbroke, without heeding the request.

"I don't care whether you like it or not. It is plain enough that we ought to do something when a man is trying to kill another. Bring out the tiller!"

Mr. Millweed obeyed the order this time. Dory took the tiller, and placed it at his side, where it would be ready for use if the occasion should require.

"There is a round stick by the centre-board casing. You had better have that in your hand, for you may want to defend yourself before we get through with this business. I don't know what the quarrel is about; but we are likely to find out very soon," added Dory.

"Help! Help! Murder!"

"There it is again!" exclaimed the skipper, not a little excited by this time.

"It's awful, isn't it, Dory?" added Bolingbroke, his teeth chattering with terror at the terrible sounds that were borne over the dark waters.

"Juniper, ahoy!" screamed Dory, forming a speaking-trumpet with his two hands. "What's the matter?"

No reply came back in answer to the question. Just then Dory began to wonder whether or not these cries were not a trick to call the Goldwing out from her hiding-place. The wind had just breezed up; and Tim Lingerwell might fear that the fugitive would escape him, after all his labor and pains to capture him.

He thought enough of the idea to mention it to his passenger. Bolingbroke was ready to adopt the opinion that it was a trick: he was ready to adopt any thing rather than go near the Juniper, whether there was a fight or not on board of her.

"Of course it is a ruse to get you out of your hiding-place," said he with energy. "I thought of that myself."

"If the wind hadn't just breezed up, I should

not have thought of such a thing," added Dory, still musing upon the point; for he did not like the idea of having his passenger taken from the Goldwing by a trick.

On the other hand, it was possible, perhaps probable, that the two men had fallen out, and come to blows. Dory knew that Lingerwell was a bad man, and it is always easy for such men to make trouble. Strange as it may seem, the skipper did not connect the large sum of money in his hip-pocket with the quarrel on board of the Juniper. He did not even think of the bills he had taken from the steam-launch in the absence of her crew.

"I wouldn't go near her, Dory," argued Bolingbroke. "I hope you won't step into the trap Tim has set for you to fall into."

"I am not afraid of Tim Lingerwell, and I am going over there to see if any thing is the matter. We will be a little cautious about approaching the steamer."

"But you can't run away from her if you find it is only a trick," reasoned Bolingbroke.

"We must take our chances," replied Dory.

By this time the Goldwing was entering the

passage between Cedar and Garden Islands. The Juniper was close to the shore, and the islands were about the eighth of a mile apart. The wind was freshening every minute; and Dory decided to run by the steamer, going as near as it was prudent to go.

He could still hear the voices of the two men, though their tone had greatly changed. The skipper saw that the steamer was still at anchor, for she had swung around with her head to the wind. He was satisfied, by this fact, that the call for help was not a trick: if it had been, the Juniper would have been under way by this time.

"Juniper, ahoy!" called Dory, as the Goldwing came up with the launch. "What is the matter on board?"

"Nothing is the matter. Greeze has had the nightmare, and shouted murder in his sleep," replied Lingerwell, trying to laugh it off, though the effort was a very sickly one.

"Help! help!" shouted the engineer from the other end of the boat.

"He don't seem to have got over his nightmare yet," added Dory. — "What is the matter there? What ails you?" demanded the skipper.

"Lingerwell has nearly killed me: he says I stole his money while he was after the Millweed fellow," replied Greeze.

"Shut up, you stupid blockhead! Silence! Don't say another word about it, and we will fix up the matter," said Lingerwell in a wheedling tone, as though he would have given something handsome to have sealed the lips of the engineer.

"I won't shut up! I have been insulted and abused; and I will have satisfaction if it costs me my life. I didn't take your money. I didn't know you had any," growled Greeze, moving aft.

This explanation on the part of the engineer enabled Dory to understand the nature of the quarrel between the two men. When the Juniper had anchored, Lingerwell had evidently taken the pocket-book from its hiding-place, and found that worthless paper had been put in the place of the four hundred and fifty dollars. As he was not aware that Dory, or any other person, had been on board, he naturally concluded that the engineer must have robbed him of his ill-gotten money.

Dory had come up into the wind under the lee of the Juniper. The lantern hung on a stanchion in the after part of the steamer, so that the skipper or the Goldwing and his passenger could see what took place on board of her. The engineer had no sooner reached the place where Lingerwell stood, than he leaped upon him with the fury of a tiger.

CHAPTER VI.

THE IMPULSIVE ASSAULT OF THE ENGINEER.

THE engineer was evidently suffering under the humiliation of his former defeat; and now he was seeking to satisfy his revengeful feelings rather than gain any point, for Lingerwell had offered to "fix up the matter." His onslaught was so sudden and unexpected that Lingerwell was borne down beneath him.

Dory was wise enough to see, on the instant, that the impulsive attack of the engineer was a great mistake; but it was too late to correct it. In this case his sympathies were not "with the bottom dog;" for the engineer had the right on his side, in spite of his blunder.

The skipper of the Goldwing felt called upon to take a hand in the conflict; and, when Lingerwell was about to shake off his opponent, he went to the assistance of the latter. The engineer had thrown his man upon his face, and he was in the act of turning over when Dory put his knees on the back of the fallen one.

"Put your foot on his back, and grab one of his hands!" exclaimed Dory, as he grasped an arm.

"I can hold him! He tried to kill me, and I will get even with him!" gasped Greeze.

"Dont hurt him," added Dory.

"I will pay him off for what he did to me!" cried the engineer.

"If you strike him, or kick him, I will leave at once!" added Dory decidedly. "We can hold him, and keep him from harming you again."

"He abused me, and I will get even with him," replied Greeze, a little mollified by the threat of Dory; for he saw that he could not manage the steamer alone.

"Don't harm him: the law will punish him," continued Dory. "Bolly."

The passenger in the Goldwing had been looking on with no little surprise and terror, and had not ventured upon the deck of the Juniper. Possibly he was too much alarmed to realize that the tables had been turned.

"What is it, Dory?" he responded to the call.

"Bring me the rope that lies under the tiller."

Bolingbroke found the line, and carried it to

the skipper; but he was careful not to go too near the fallen tiger, for such he had proved to be to him. Dory took the line, and succeeded in making it fast to the arm of Lingerwell.

"What are you about, you young villain? Do you mean to tie my hands?" demanded the fallen man.

"That's the idea exactly," replied Dory, as he attempted to pass the line around the arm held by the engineer.

Lingerwell had been quiet for a minute after Dory took hold of him, but the idea of being captured and tied up like a felon was too much for him. With a series of heavy oaths, he made a desperate effort to shake off his assailants. The engineer meant business, though the direction of the assault had been taken out of his hands by the new-comer. He lay down upon his victim, and jammed his knees into the small of his back, so that escape was impossible. Dory passed the line around the other wrist of the conspirator, and the two were securely bound together behind him.

"He is all right now, and cannot harm anybody," said Dory. "Get another line, and we will secure his feet." Bolingbroke brought the rope, for by this time he could see that his great enemy was powerless.

Dory fastened the feet of Lingerwell together, and then turned him on his side, so that he could be more comfortable. Again the victim struggled to loose himself; but Dory had done his work well, and he could produce no impression upon the rope.

"This is an outrage!" yelled he, furious with passion.

"I suppose it isn't an outrage to try to kill a man," replied Dory, as he took the lantern and examined the fastenings he had put on the prisoner.

"I didn't try to kill him! That is all nonsense!" replied Lingerwell, suspending his struggles.

"We won't argue the matter now," replied Dory, walking to the forward part of the boat.

He was followed by the engineer, who seemed to be desirous to explain the affair. Doubtless he was grateful for the service the boy had rendered to him, and looked upon the skipper of the Goldwing as his friend.

"You are a plucky boy, Dory," said Greeze, when they reached the wheel, near the bow of the boat. "But I think I could have handled that fellow alone."

"It is very strange that you should get into a quarrel out here in the middle of the night," added Dory.

"It wasn't a quarrel of my making; and, if he hadn't taken me when I was not thinking of such a thing, the boot would have been on the other leg. He's bigger than I am, but I can handle him if I have fair play."

"How did you happen to get into such a row?"

"I stopped the boat when we reached this place, and then let go the anchor, at Lingerwell's order. When I went forward, I found him on the floor, feeling about under the ceiling. I didn't know what he was doing; and he didn't care to have me know, for he told me to go aft and bank the fire in the furnace. I did so, and when I got through I went forward again. Lingerwell was at the lantern, looking over what was in a big pocket-book he had in his hands."

"Had he said any thing about a pocket-book before?" asked Dory.

"Not a word. When I got to him, he looked as though he was very nervous and excited. He poked the pocket-book over, and then fished his pockets all through. I asked him what the matter was. He said he had dropped his pocket-book on the floor, some time during the day; he didn't know when. He had just found it; but the money had all been taken out, and a piece of newspaper put in its place to swell it out."

"Did he say how much money was in it?" inquired Dory.

"He said there was a good deal in it, but he didn't tell me how much."

"Did he say there was a hundred dollars or more?"

"He didn't say a word about it. He kept getting more excited, and at last he said I must have taken the money from the pocket-book. I answered, that I didn't do it: I hadn't seen his pocket-book, and didn't know he had any money with him. On that he got mad, and I was as mad as he was.

"We had a long jaw about it, and then he pitched into me. He got me by the throat before I knew what he was about. He put me down, and then tried to fish my pockets. I yelled for help, for I thought he would kill me. I hardly knew what I did; but I shook him off, and we had another savage jaw about it. Then he pitched into me again. He had a club in his hand; and I think he would have used it on me, if he hadn't heard you yell just at this time."

"I hoped my hail would let him know there was some one at hand, though it was only a boy," added Dory.

"That was what made him let up on me. Then he tried to smooth it over; but I never was treated like that before, and I meant to have it out with him."

"Well, here we are; and what is to be done next?" asked Dory.

"We were waiting down here to catch that Millweed fellow that stole the money from the safe," replied Greeze.

"He says he didn't take the money from the safe, and he is going back to Burlington to face the music."

"We might as well go along then: we haven't any more business up here. You can steer the Juniper, and we will tow the Goldwing," suggested the engineer. "I don't know how this thing is coming out, but I am ready to go to Burlington. I suppose Lingerwell will have me discharged after this, but I don't care for that. You have tied him hand and foot, and I don't know what you mean by that. I meant to take what I owed him out of his hide."

"I tied him to keep him from pitching into you again. I want to see Mr. Longbrook as soon as we get to Burlington; and he can do what he likes with him," replied Dory. "We will start for Burlington as soon as you are ready."

When the excitement was over, Bolingbroke Millweed had returned to the Goldwing, and to his berth in the cabin, where he was now fast asleep. The engineer replenished his fire, and in half an hour the Juniper was under way. At four o'clock in the morning she was at her wharf in Burlington. The Goldwing was made fast alongside of her. It was nearly daylight, and it would be quite by the time Dory could reach the residence of Mr. Longbrook.

Bolingbroke was roused from his slumbers in the cabin, but he objected to calling upon the storekeeper at so early an hour in the morning.

Dory did not care for his opinion, and insisted upon going without any delay. Greeze was to keep watch over Lingerwell until he heard from Dory, and Mr. Longbrook was to decide what was to be done with the prisoner.

The house of the storekeeper was easily found. It was about five by this time, and the early visitors saw that the people were up. To Dory's inquiry for the head of the family, the servant said he had gone to the store. He had staid there till midnight the night before, and had left the house as soon as it was light.

Dory was not a little astonished at this severe devotion to business; but he hastened to the store, and found Mr. Longbrook was busy over his books. He had locked himself in, but he opened the door in answer to the skipper's vigorous knocks.

"I am too busy to see any one now," said the storekeeper impatiently. "Come at nine o'clock, and I will see you."

"This young man wants to see you at once," added Dory, pulling Bolingbroke into the doorway.

"What, Millweed! So you have come back,

young man," added Mr. Longbrook, as he recognized his late assistant.

"I have come back to tell you, sir, that I did not take the money from your safe," stammered Bolingbroke.

"What did you run away for, then?" demanded the merchant severely.

"Because I was a fool and was frightened. I found that Mr. Lingerwell was determined to convict me, guilty or innocent; and I had not the courage to stay and see it out," replied Bolingbroke honestly.

"You lost four hundred and fifty dollars from your safe, Mr. Longbrook," interposed Dory.

"That was just the amount taken, and this young fellow took it. It looks as though he came to work here at this time for the purpose of getting it, and he left as soon as he had the money," said the merchant angrily. "What have you done with the money, you young rascal?"

"I have not had it, I have not seen it," protested Bolingbroke.

"Don't tell me that! No one else could have taken it. You and Lingerwell were the only two persons who went to the safe."

"Possibly Mr. Lingerwell took it himself," suggested Dory.

Mr. Longbrook knit his brows into a frown, and turned away as though he was thinking of something. Doubtless he was considering whether or not it was possible that his trusted head man could have done such a deed.

"At any rate here is the money," added Dory, pulling the roll of bills from his pocket.

The merchant opened his eyes very wide, and so did Mr. Bolingbroke Millweed.

CHAPTER VII.

BOLINGBROKE MILLWEED OUT OF A PLACE.

MR. LONGBROOK took the bills, and a smile of satisfaction overspread his troubled face. He looked at Dory with astonishment, and then glanced from him to Bolingbroke. The latter was quite as much surprised as the owner of the four hundred and fifty dollars.

Dory had not given a hint to his companion or to the engineer that he had the money. He had concealed the fact from prudential motives. He had told his mother all about it, but he was not inclined to lead either of his associates in the boat into temptation.

"I see," said Mr. Longbrook, nodding his head at Dory. "Your friend has concluded to give up the money, and expects me to say nothing more about it."

"I never saw the money before; and I didn't know till this minute that Dory had it," protested Bolingbroke earnestly.

"He tells the exact truth," added Dory. "Neither he nor any one but my mother, who is at Genverres, knew that I had the money. I think you had better hear the whole story, and then you can judge for yourself."

Mr. Longbrook was quite willing to hear the story, for he was deeply interested by this time. He asked Dory and his companion into the store, and locked the door again. Bolingbroke gave his part of the narrative first, and Dory finished it out.

"I believed Bolingbroke told me the truth; and I accepted Mr. Lingerwell's statement that one of the two must have stolen the money," said Dory. "When the skipper and engineer left the Juniper to catch my passenger, I looked the steamer over, and found the pocket-book. I put the piece of newspaper into the place where I took out the bills, hoping that Mr. Lingerwell would suppose he had the bills until he got to Burlington."

Then followed the skipper's account of the quarrel on board of the Juniper, which confirmed Dory's statement. It was as clear to the merchant as it was to Dory, that the head man had stolen the money.

"Where is Lingerwell now?" asked Mr. Longbrook.

"He is on board of the Juniper, tied hand and foot; and the engineer is keeping guard over him. He did not know I had been on board of the Juniper in his absence; and he was sure that Greeze must have taken the money from the pocket-book, and put the newspaper in its place. You can do what you like with him."

"I knew that man was a villain!" exclaimed Bolingbroke when Dory had finished his explanation. "I saw why I was sent to the safe for the cash-book, when it was almost within reach of his hands; and that was one of my reasons for running away. I was a fool, but I was frightened."

"I wish I had known that Lingerwell was a rascal a little sooner. Since he went after this young man yesterday, I have been examining my books. I am satisfied that he has robbed me of hundreds, if not thousands, of dollars. I can see just how he has done it. Now we will go down and see him, and we will have a warrant for his arrest.

By this time it was seven o'clock, and the merchant departed for the warrant and the officer to serve it. Dory and Bolingbroke went with him.

As they passed the Van Ness House, Dory was not a little surprised to see his uncle standing at the entrance of the hotel with quite a little crowd of boys. The skipper counted ten of them, and he wondered if they were to be pupils in the Beech-Hill Industrial School.

"You are here in good time, Theodore," demanded Captain Gildrock, as he recognized his nephew.

"I came up on a little business, uncle," replied Dory.

"Very important business it was to me, Captain Gildrock," added Mr. Longbrook. "I am under very great obligations to him."

The breakfast-bell rang, and the boys were sent in to obtain the morning meal. The merchant gave an outline of the loss and recovery of his money. The captain asked a great many questions, which were all answered to his satisfaction. Then he insisted that the party should breakfast with him.

Mr. Longbrook accepted the invitation, and they entered the hotel. In the vestibule the merchant met the justice to whom he intended to apply for the warrant. He stated his case to him, and the gentleman promised to have the warrant ready by the time he had finished his breakfast. The party seated themselves at the table.

"A telegram for you, Captain Gildrock," said one of the clerks, bringing the message to him.

"'Dory away; no pilot; cannot go up the lake. — JEPSON,'" read the captain from the despatch in his hand. "Then you did not come down in the Sylph, Theodore. Of course you did not. I have heard the story of your movements during the night. I telegraphed to you last night from here to come down in the steamer, and take the new scholars to Beech Hill."

"I have the Goldwing here, and I can take them home in her," replied Dory.

"But I have ten boys with me: there they are at the other table. They are about as wild and harum-scarum a set of youngsters as I ever saw in my life. But we will take all that out of them in a few days, when I get them to Beech Hill," replied the captain confidently.

"I can take the crowd up in the Goldwing."

"We will see about that when we have done breakfast, and you have disposed of your prisoner."

"The Juniper is at your service, Captain Gildrock."

"Thank you: perhaps we may want to use her."

Mr. Longbrook inquired in regard to the sloop that had been sunk. It was not likely that Lingerwell would be able to pay for the mischief he had done; and the merchant said he had a sloop, not a very fine one, which he was willing to give as a substitute for the one lost. Bolingbroke was delighted with this offer, and promptly accepted it.

After breakfast the party proceeded to the wharf where the Juniper lay, the recruits for the Industrial School being required to report at the hotel at ten o'clock. Mr. Longbrook found things on board of his steam-launch precisely as represented to him by Dory. Lingerwell still lay on the floor in the after part of the steamer. Greeze sat near him, and apparently had not taken his eye off him since the departure of Dory early in the morning.

The officer with the warrant had not yet put in an appearance. The merchant, before he showed himself to his delinquent head man, called the engineer up the wharf, and questioned him in regard to the events of the night. His statement did not vary from that of Dory and Bolingbroke, though Greeze as yet had no suspicion that the money he had been charged with stealing had been taken from the safe of his employer.

"I think there are enough of us to handle this man," said Mr. Longbrook, as he returned to the steam-launch. "You may untie his hands, Greeze."

"With fair play I can handle him alone," replied the engineer, as he proceeded to release the wrists of the culprit on the floor. Greeze helped him to get upon his feet, and then gave him a seat opposite the merchant.

"Well, Lingerwell, I find you did not capture the thief," said the storekeeper.

"I did not: he found an accomplice in Dory Dornwood, who helped him to escape," replied the prisoner doggedly; and, as he had no knowledge of what had transpired at the store, he was not prepared to admit any thing.

"But how does it happen that I find you a prisoner, bound hand and foot?" asked the merchant.

"I am the victim of an outrage. I had some difficulty with the engineer in the night, and he joined forces with Dory against me. By taking me unawares, they succeeded in making me a prisoner. I had some money with me, and dropped my pocket-book on the floor near the wheel. When I found it, the money was taken out, and its place filled with a piece of newspaper." This statement also confirmed that of Dory.

"How much money did you happen to have with you?" inquired his employer.

"About a hundred dollars. Of course I knew that the engineer had done this, for no one but Greeze and myself had been on board of the steamer."

"Are you sure of that?"

"As sure as I can be of any thing in this world," persisted Lingerwell.

"Are you correct about the amount of money in your pocket-book?"

"I would not say there was just a hundred dollars in it, but about that amount."

"Wasn't there four hundred and fifty dollars in the pocket-book?" demanded the merchant sharply.

"I am sure there was not," the culprit persisted.

"The pocket-book was not taken by the thief:

do you happen to have it about you, Lingerwell?"

"After I found it was empty, I laid it on the rail for a minute, and it fell overboard. It was so dark I could not recover it," replied the prisoner.

While Lingerwell was inventing and uttering this falsehood, Mr. Longbrook picked up a piece of newspaper, folded in the shape of a bank-bill, which he found lying on the floor of the steamer.

"I suppose this is the piece of paper you found in the pocket-book in place of the money?"

"That is the piece of paper."

"Here is the rest of the paper," added Dory, taking a newspaper from his pocket.

The merchant put the two pieces of paper together, and found they were part of the same sheet.

"Then it was this Dory that robbed me of my money!" exclaimed the prisoner savagely.

"Robbed you of my money, you mean, Lingerwell. Dory has returned to me the money he took from the pocket-book you hid under the ceiling of the launch. Lingerwell, to the crime of robbery you add the meanness and the baseness of charging it upon an innocent person," said the merchant sternly. "Yesterday I would have trusted you with all I had in the world. To-day I find you are a thief and a villain. Here comes the officer with a warrant for you."

Lingerwell subsided at once; in fact, he broke down like a child, and cried like a baby. He had not supposed he could be discovered so readily, but rogues are very apt to make blunders. The officer marched him to the lockup; and we may as well add here, that he was sentenced, in due time, to the State prison for three years.

"I suppose I shall be wanted in the store, Mr. Longbrook?" asked Bolingbroke, when the culprit had been marched off.

"If you had not run away, you would have been all right, young man," replied the merchant. "Yesterday I engaged two experienced men at very low wages, and they were to come this morning. I shall not need you."

"If it is a fair question, Mr. Longbrook, how much do you pay the two men?" asked Captain Gildrock.

"One five, and the other six, dollars a week."

The captain nodded his head, but made no reply.

"The fact is, there are three times as many clerks as there are places," added the storekeeper.

Bolingbroke was terribly disappointed to lose even a temporary place.

CHAPTER VIII.

PUPILS FOR THE BEECH-HILL INDUSTRIAL SCHOOL.

MR. LONGBROOK conducted Bolingbroke to another part of the wharf, and pointed out to him an old sloop, about the size of the one sunk in the deep water.

"I am sorry you are out of a place, young man; but you are welcome to that boat in place of the one you lost, though I don't feel under any obligations to replace it. It was your misfortune that you were accused of a crime. If you had not run away, I should have had a chance to investigate the matter. I went out for a moment, and when I returned you had gone. When I want another clerk, I will try to think of you," said the merchant, as he walked away towards the store.

Bolingbroke could hardly keep from crying at his disappointment in losing the place, which he had expected would be a permanent one. The salary was only four dollars a week; but he could board with a relative for two, and he could at least relieve his father of one mouth to feed.

"What's the matter, my lad?" asked Captain Gildrock, as he and Dory walked up the wharf. "You look as though you had not a friend in the world."

"I have lost the place I expected to have, and my father is very poor," replied Bolingbroke with due humility.

"What sort of a place was it?" asked the captain.

"It was a situation in Mr. Longbrook's store. I have been looking for a place for a year; but I am afraid I shall never find one," replied Bolingbroke, hoping the rich man would interest himself in his favor.

"There are ten clerks for every vacancy. Can't you find any thing else to do?"

"I don't know: I never looked for any other kind of a place."

"I should think you might find a place to work on a farm," added the captain in perfect good faith.

"On a farm!" exclaimed Bolingbroke, actually stopping in his walk in his astonishment.

"I hear that there is a scarcity of help on the farms in the State," continued Captain Gildrock. "I should say you might earn four or five dollars a week, or at least fifteen dollars a month, on a farm, besides your board; and that is better pay than you can get in a store."

"I never worked on a farm," added Bolingbroke, who possibly knew that the rich man of Beech Hill had some peculiar notions.

"Where do you live?"

"I live in Genverres, on the north side, where my father has a farm."

"Does your father carry on a farm?"

"Yes, sir: he has always been a farmer."

"I should think you could find enough to do at home. Don't your father need any help on his place?"

"He hires all the help he wants. I never did any thing on the farm."

"You look like a stout fellow; and I should think you could do a man's work for him," added the captain, surprised in his turn.

"Perhaps I could, if I had been brought up to it," replied Bolingbroke rather sheepishly.

"Have you any brothers and sisters?"

"One brother and two sisters."

"I should not think your father ought to be very poor, if he has a farm, and two stout boys to help him. What does your brother do?"

"He has been looking for a place in a store for the last three years. He has tried in Burlington, Rutland, and Brattleboro'; and he thinks of going to New York or Boston."

"Don't your brother work on the farm when he is out of work?" asked Captain Gildrock, who was beginning to get an inkling of the situation.

"Neither of us ever did any thing on the farm. Mother has never been willing that we should work on a farm," replied Bolingbroke. "Father wants us to do something else."

"Do your two sisters do any thing? How old are they?"

"Elinora is twenty, and Fatima is twenty-two. They have never done any thing."

"I dare say they are both engaged, and their future is marked out," suggested the captain with a smile.

"Neither of them is engaged, and there is nothing to indicate their future."

"I suppose you have all been to school?"

"We are all graduates of the Genverres high-school."

"Indeed!" exclaimed Captain Gildrock significantly, as though the last item of information explained the situation fully to him. "Why don't you learn a trade?"

"Learn a trade!" ejaculated Bolingbroke. "I never thought of such a thing."

"It is a good time to think of it now then. You are not more than sixteen or seventeen," suggested the captain. "If you like, I will receive you as a pupil in the Beech-Hill Industrial School, where you can become a carpenter or a machinist, or learn to run an engine. You can stay for a year or longer, and it will cost you nothing. I think you said your father was very poor, and no other member of the family seems to be earning any thing."

"My father has hard work to get along. His farm is mortgaged for about all it is worth, and it takes all the money he can raise to pay the interest; and he is afraid he will lose all his property."

"If you will come to my school, I will put you in the way of saving money enough from your wages another year to pay your father's interest. If I don't I will pay it myself."

"I think a word from you would get me a place in some store in Burlington. If you would recommend me" —

"How can I recommend you when I never saw you before in my life? I don't do things in that way," interposed Captain Gildrock. "If you join the school, I will see that you are in a position to earn fair wages another year. One of our last year's boys gets thirty dollars a month besides his board. All of them get twenty or more. After they have had experience they will command from fifty to a hundred dollars a month. You can think of it, and let me know your decision in a few days; for the school opens on the 1st of September."

The party reached the hotel by this time. Dory and Bolingbroke were summoned to appear as witnesses in the case of Lingerwell the next day. Captain Gildrock found the ten recruits for the school at the hotel. He had picked them up among his friends in Montpelier, St. Albans, and St. Johnsbury. If he did not know it before, he had ascertained on his trip to Burlington with them, that they were a set of wild boys.

He was in a hurry to get them to Beech Hill before they tore any houses down, or did any other mischief. At least five out of the ten had been expelled from private schools or academies, because the instructors could not manage them; three of them were the sons of wealthy men; and all of them were supposed to have a liking for mechanical pursuits. The captain was confident that he could manage them after he got them to his estate.

Dory was satisfied that he could seat them all in the Goldwing, for he had often taken out twenty in her on pleasure-excursions. But his uncle was afraid they would "cut up," as he expressed himself, and make trouble on the passage. He spoke to them about going in the schooner, and they were delighted with the idea. Most of them had never been on the lake in any sort of a craft, and some had never even seen a steamboat or a sailboat.

Captain Gildrock consented to the arrangement after he had charged the recruits to behave with propriety in the boat, and to obey the orders of the skipper. They promised to do these things, and they were marched down to the wharf. Bolingbroke followed the party, evidently because he did not know what else to do with himself.

"Couldn't you say a word to your uncle in my favor, Dory?" said he on the way to the lake. "He knows all the storekeepers, and a word from him would make a place for me."

"He won't recommend you, because he knows nothing at all about you," replied Dory. "Why don't you join the school, as he asked you to do?"

"I should make nothing for my father by doing that," added Bolingbroke. "I want to help him pay his interest-money."

"How much can you do for him when you get only four dollars a week?" asked Dory. "You would have to pay three for your board, and that would leave you about fifty to pay for your clothes, washing, and all other expenses. You would be just as well off at the end of the year, and so would your father, if you went to the school."

"But the idea of becoming a carpenter or a greasy machinist!" exclaimed Bolingbroke with a curl upon his lip.

"I thought you wanted to earn money to help your father. A little oil on your hands won't hurt you," replied Dory, rather disgusted with his companion.

"I am sure my mother won't let me become a mechanic, but I will speak to her about it to-night. I suppose I can go down with you in the Goldwing: I have no other way to get home."

"Certainly, I have room enough. But how will you get the sloop Mr. Longbrook gave you up to Genverres?"

"I will write to Sim Green, and he can go up in her when he is ready to return."

When the party arrived at the wharf, and the Goldwing was pointed out to them, they were delighted with her. Some of them wondered if it were safe to go in her, though most of the ten were afraid of nothing. Captain Gildrock had business in Burlington which would detain him till the next day, and it was arranged that Dory should come down in the Sylph to attend court. His uncle would return in the steamer.

"But what are we to do with all these fellows before you come, uncle Royal?" asked Dory. "They will tear the house down, and dry up the lake."

"Jepson and Brookbine are there; and, as they

are to instruct the pupils, they ought to be able to manage them," replied the captain; but his looks indicated that he had some anxiety about the matter. "Tell Mr. Brookbine to assign the rooms to the boys, one to each, in the dormitory. The rogues will not think of doing any mischief until they are better acquainted."

Captain Gildrock gave Dory a paper on which were written the names of the new pupils. He called them off, one at a time, and gave to each one his place in the boat. They behaved very well under the eye of the captain. They were seated five on each side of the standing-room, leaving room for the skipper to go forward and aft.

"I suppose you know all about a boat, fellows," said Dory, as he went forward to hoist the jib.

"Never saw a sailboat before!" exclaimed Ben Ludlow.

"Nor I!" shouted half a dozen others.

"Where have you been all your lives?" laughed Dory, as he paused on his way.

"In the woods," replied Ben.

The skipper shoved off, and the Goldwing stood across the lake.

CHAPTER IX.

THE VOLUNTEER HELMSMAN AND HIS MOVEMENTS.

THE wind was strong from the south-west; and, after passing the breakwater, the Goldwing struck into a smart little sea for a fresh-water pond. The motion was so strange, not to say exciting, to the passengers from the interior, that they kept very still for a time. The water slopped over the bow, and occasionally a bucketful pounded pretty hard on the forward deck.

Some of the boys were evidently a little startled, though they did not like to show that they were moved by this new experience. Others tried to look and act as though they had been on the waves all the days of their lives.

"It's all right, fellows," said Dory, when about half a barrel of water slapped on the boards forward. "We intend to keep on the top of the water."

"Does a boat always do like that, and take the

water in?" asked Ben Ludlow, who had never seen a sheet of water bigger than a pond a mile in diameter.

"No: sometimes the boat don't throw the water at all, but sometimes it does ten times as bad as now. I have been out in this boat when one hand had to keep baling all the time. We call this a quiet sail."

"Of course it's a quiet sail," added Oscar Chester, who had once been on a steamer. "There isn't any thing to be afraid of."

"I can stand it as long as the rest of you," replied Ben Ludlow, who thought the last speaker had cast an imputation upon his courage. "When Dory is frightened, it will be time enough for the rest of us to get scared."

"I had no idea that a boat made such a fuss in going along," said Dave Windsor.

"It don't always; but we are sailing against the wind as near as we can go," Dory explained. "I suppose all you fellows are going to learn how to sail a boat, and you might as well begin now."

The skipper of the Goldwing proceeded to show in what manner the mouth of Beaver River was to be reached. When he had gone far enough to weather Willsborough Point, he could lay his course to Thompson's Point; and from there he must beat about dead to windward. Most of the new pupils were interested, and asked a great many questions. Dory explained every thing very minutely; and it was not his fault if they did not understand, at least the theory of sailing a boat against the wind.

"But I can't see what makes the boat go ahead when the wind is against her," suggested John Brattle. "I can understand how the wind pushes the boat along when it is blowing from behind her, but not when it comes from the way it does now."

"It is the friction of the wind against the sails. Did you ever see a ferry-boat cross a river by the force of the current?"

John Brattle happened to be the only one of the party who had seen a current-boat. He had crossed the Androscoggin River, in Maine, in a stage on such a craft.

"If the ferry-boat were headed square across the river, the current would not move her any way but down the river," added Dory.

"There was a big wire rope stretched across the

river, which did not let her go down the stream," replied John Brattle. "Then the boat was turned to an angle half-way between the direction of the current and the wire rope."

"Precisely as our sails are set at an angle with the course of the boat. In this position the friction of the water against the boat forces it across the river."

"But you have no wire rope."

"We have a centre-board instead." Dory pointed out the centre-board of the Goldwing, and showed how it worked. "This boat would slide off sideways if it were not for that."

"But we have to go a great deal farther when beating," said Ned Bellows.

"Of course we do," replied Dory. "Sometimes we have to go two miles to make one when the wind is dead ahead."

"Captain Gildrock said it was twenty miles from Burlington to Beech Hill. Must we go forty miles to get there?" asked Ben Ludlow.

"Not at all: the wind isn't dead ahead. Here we are, just north of Willsborough Point. I am coming about now. Look out for your heads when the boom goes over."

Dory put the helm down, and all the sails began to flap and bang. But in a moment the Goldwing took the wind on the starboard tack, the sails went over, and the schooner began to gather headway on her new course.

"That's what we call tacking," said the skipper. "We shall go about eleven miles on this tack."

"I say, Dory, let me steer her a while now," added Oscar Chester, rising from his seat, and moving aft.

"Keep your seat!" replied the skipper rather sharply. "You mustn't move about in the boat."

"But I want to steer her," persisted Oscar, resuming his seat.

"Did you ever steer a boat?" asked Dory.

"I never steered a sailboat; but I can do it as well as you can," added the new pupil. "I have seen just how it is done. When you want the boat to go to the right, you put the stick in your hand to the left."

"I don't believe in running any risks in a boat, and I must keep the helm myself," answered Dory. "There is wind enough to upset the boat if you don't know how to handle her."

"But I do know how to handle her. I have kept my eyes open, and I know all about it. It don't take me a month to learn any thing."

"If we were alone I would let you try it, just to enable you to see how easy it is to be mistaken," said Dory, laughing.

"It's nothing to steer a boat! You needn't make such a big thing of it."

"Well, it is a big thing!" exclaimed Bolingbroke. "I thought I knew something about it yesterday, and I got overboard in two hundred and fifty feet of water; and that is deep enough to drown the whole of you. I should have finished my mortal career then if Dory had not picked me up."

None of the other boys said any thing, though it was plain to the skipper that they did not want Oscar to steer the boat. Dory began to understand what sort of a fellow Oscar was; and it was evident to him that he was the bully of the crowd, and that he had already set up, and perhaps established, his superiority. He was older and larger than Dory, though three or four of the new pupils were heavier than he.

"You all seem to be afraid of a boat," continued

Oscar with a palpable sneer. "I am not afraid of her."

"Can you swim a mile?" asked Dory quietly.

"I can't swim a rod. I don't intend to tip her over."

"Perhaps the rest of the fellows can swim."

They all protested that they could not.

"If this boat should fill with water, she would go to the bottom like a pound of lead," continued Dory. "The water is over two hundred feet deep out here. It is four hundred off Thompson's Point. But, if you can't swim, you would drown just as quick in six feet of water as in six hundred."

"I don't care for your bugbears: I'm not afraid of them. I want to steer this boat, and I'm going to do it!" added Oscar stoutly.

"I don't believe you will steer her on this trip," replied Dory in a quiet tone. "But I will give you a chance to steer all you want to when we are alone."

"Do you take me for a little chicken, Dory, that can be led around by you?" demanded Oscar, rising from his place.

"Keep your seat!" added the skipper sharply.

"No, I won't keep my seat! I will let you know that you are not my boss."

"In a boat all hands must obey the skipper, as I shall obey you, Oscar Chester, when you are the skipper of any boat I am in; and that is just what Captain Gildrock told you all to do just before we sailed."

"I don't obey a little snipper-snapper of a fellow like you, Dory. I never was bossed by any boy, and I don't begin now," blustered Oscar, moving towards the stern of the boat.

Dory saw that there was likely to be trouble. He had correctly read the character of Chester; and he was not anxious, while responsible for the safety of the boat and her passengers, to have any difficulty with him. He was not afraid of him, bold and stout as Oscar appeared to be.

Putting the helm up a little, he allowed the schooner to fall off until the strong wind heeled the boat over, so that the water was nearly even with the top of the wash-board. This was decidedly startling to some of the boys, who cried out in their alarm.

The Goldwing went over so far that Oscar was not at all secure in his footing; and he came very near tumbling over the heads of the fellows on the lee side, for they had bent forward as the schooner heeled over.

"Sit down! Keep your seat, Oscar Chester!" shouted Dory. But it was no part of the rebel's nature to obey an order of any kind after what had happened. The inside of the boat was rather crowded, except on each side of the tiller, where the space had been reserved for the helmsman.

Making a lively spring for the open space on the lee side of the rudder-head, he brought up on the seat, just as the skipper put the helm down to bring the boat back to her former course. The Goldwing was jumping on the waves; and the rebel did not fetch up just as he intended, for the motion of the boat interfered with his calculations. He grasped the main-sheet, and finally came down on the bit of deck astern of the standing-room.

Oscar evidently wanted to prove that he "always came down-stairs that way;" for he let go the sheet, and tried to stand up straight. His pride was still in the ascendency. Dory had put the helm over so far that the sails were spilled, and this set the schooner to pitching. Oscar had hardly let go the sheet, when he lost his balance, and pitched into the lake, disappearing beneath the surface. Dory tried to catch him before he went over, but failed to do so.

"He has fallen over into the water!" screamed some of the boys, terribly frightened by this time.

"He will be drowned!" yelled others.

The only one who had not entirely lost his head was the skipper. Dory was as cool as though he had been up to his neck in ice-water. He had been in all sorts of scrapes, though he had never encountered a bully under such unfavorable circumstances. He had put the helm down before, and the Goldwing had lost her headway. Of course she would not answer her helm when she had lost her steerage-way.

Oscar Chester came to the top of the water, and all the boys shouted. Dory did not even look at him, for he was busy with the boat. He filled away, and came about as soon as he got steerage-way. Oscar was floundering about in the most unreasonable manner, with a better chance of being drowned than of being saved.

CHAPTER X.

THE BATTLE NEAR GARDEN ISLAND.

OSCAR CHESTER had disappeared a second time, and most of the boys in the boat were paralyzed with terror. Dory saw him as he rose, and knew just where he was. The Goldwing worked lively in that breeze. The skipper handled his sheets with extraordinary celerity. Going free, the schooner dashed down to the spot, and reached it just as the victim of his own folly rose again to the surface.

Dory saw him just as the bow of the Goldwing was about to strike his head. Keeping her off a little, he leaned over the side, and grasped the drowning bully by the hair of the head, though not till he had put the helm hard down.

It was but a meagre hold that he had upon the sufferer, but he clung to him till the boat came up into the wind. Oscar had not lost his senses, though his mouth was too full of water to permit any utterance, if he had any thing to say. Dory held on, though the aimless struggles of the victim rendered it very difficult for him to do so.

"Grab him by the collar!" shouted Dory to the next fellow in the boat. Lew Shoreham, who was the largest boy in the crowd, obeyed the order; though it was a difficult matter for an inexperienced hand to do any thing while the boat was flopping about in the heavy sea. But Lew got hold with one hand, and Dory shifted his grasp from the hair to the collar.

After a lively struggle, with the assistance of two other boys, they succeeded in hauling Oscar into the boat. He was exhausted by his struggles in the water, and he dropped upon the floor of the standing-room as limpsy as a wet rag. Dory gave no further attention to him, but grasped the helm, and soon got the Goldwing upon her course again, so that she was steady.

"Turn him over on his stomach, and let the water run out of him," said the skipper. "Here, Bolly! Come aft! You can stand up in a boat."

Bolingbroke obeyed the order, and the victim poured out a considerable quantity of water from his mouth. Dory then directed his companions to convey the sufferer to the cabin, and put him

THE BATTLE OFF GARDEN ISLAND. Page 113.

in one of the berths, covering him with the blankets. But Oscar was not insensible, for he had only exhausted himself by his violent struggles. In half an hour he had recovered from the shock. The fresh wind made it cool on the lake, and it took all the blankets on board to warm him.

"That was a narrow escape. He had been down twice; and if he had gone down again we should not have seen him again," said Bolingbroke, as he came out of the cabin. "I think that fellow will obey orders next time."

"No, he won't!" cried Oscar, sticking his head out at the door. "It isn't the first time I have been under water, and I'm not killed yet. Dory did it on purpose to pitch me overboard, and I will get even with him!"

Perhaps all but Dory and Bolingbroke knew Oscar well enough not to be greatly surprised at this demonstration. It looked as though the lesson, which Dory hoped would cure him of his desire to handle a boat before he had learned how to do it, had been wholly lost upon the pupil. None of the party said any thing in reply to the speech, and it was plain that they stood in fear of the rebel.

In another hour, when the Goldwing was approaching Thompson's Point, Oscar was sufficiently warmed up to leave the cabin. He went aft, and seated himself quite near the skipper. He looked decidedly ugly, and Dory thought that half-drowning was not enough for him. He wondered what his uncle expected to do with such a fellow. He would be equal to a whole nest of hornets from the time the school was opened.

"I heard some one call you Dory Dornwood," said Oscar, fixing his gaze upon the skipper.

"My name is Theodore Dornwood; but they call me Dory for short," replied Dory.

"The name is all right, Dory. You have insulted me, and you have pitched me into the lake," continued Oscar, frowning like an untamed savage. "You got ahead of me before all these boys; and I am not the fellow to swallow an insult, or to pass over an injury."

Dory looked at the bully once, and then took a leisure survey of the lake ahead, and of the sails of the schooner.

"I spoke to you, Dory Dornwood: didn't you hear me?" demanded Oscar in savage tones.

"I heard all you said. I have nothing to say in reply," answered the cool skipper.

"I spoke to you, and you will answer me, or take the consequences," added Oscar. "I am not a spring chicken, as you took me to be. I said that you had insulted me, and pitched me into the lake. Do you confess that you have done so?"

"I don't confess any thing. I am in charge of this boat, and responsible for the lives of those in her," replied Dory quietly. "I don't care to talk about the matter you have brought up, just now. When we get to Beech Hill I will answer your questions, and we will settle the matter if there is any thing to settle; though I would rather have you fix it up with Captain Gildrock."

"That won't do! I settle for an insult on the spot!" stormed Oscar. He rose from his seat, and with clinched fists approached the skipper.

"We are close to the land!" shouted one of the boys forward.

"I don't care where we are! We settle this matter here and now," said Oscar, making a slight movement forward.

"Come, come!" interposed Bolingbroke. "This thing has gone far enough, Oscar. Don't you see that Dory is the skipper of the boat, and that we can't do any thing without him? Let him alone, and he says he will make it right with you when we get ashore."

"Here and now!" repeated the bully.

Dory had been running for Garden Island, where he brought up on his long tack. He understood the situation, and feared that some of the party might be drowned if Oscar Chester got the control of the boat. He heard the centre-board scraping on the sands at the bottom, though the water was nearly two hundred feet deep only a short distance from the shore of the island.

The skipper realized that his rebel passenger was about to make an assault of some kind upon him, and he put the helm hard down. The boat came up into the wind with every thing shaking. Oscar sprang upon him as he did so, but Dory was on his feet at the same instant. The waves beat smartly upon the shore of the island, and the centre-board was still grating upon the bottom.

"Do you confess that you insulted me?" demanded the bully, as he seized Dory by the collar.

"I do not confess," replied Dory. At the same instant he sprang like a tiger upon his assailant.

The skipper was accustomed to the motion of the boat, while Oscar was not. The assailant had evidently not expected so vigorous a defence. Dory shook off the grasp of Oscar, a sharp struggle ensued, and it ended almost the instant it began in a heavy splash in the water.

Dory had tumbled the bully over the stern of the boat into the lake. Those who looked on could hardly tell how it was done, for the defeat of Oscar had been accomplished almost like a flash. On the land it might have been different in the result, but in the uneasy boat the experienced hand won a quick victory.

"He is in the water again!" shouted the boys.

But he was in the water not more than half a minute, for there was not ten feet between the stern of the schooner and the island. Oscar scrambled to the shore, and made his way to the level of the island. The wind had filled the sails on the other tack, and the boat began to move ahead.

Dory saw that Oscar had made a landing on the island. Attending to the sheets, he filled away on the port tack. The Goldwing dashed ahead as though she was glad to be rid of the bully who had made so much trouble on board of her.

"Are you going to leave him there, Dory?" asked Lew Shoreham.

"Of course I am going to leave him there. He can't drown on the island; and, if I take him on board again, he may destroy the whole of us," replied Dory rather warmly. "He is the most unreasonable fellow I ever met in my life."

"But what will he do on that island?" asked Ben Ludlow.

"Repent of his folly the first thing he does, I hope," answered Dory.

"Does any one live on the island?" inquired Jim Alburgh.

"No one lives there. If any one did, that fellow would get up a quarrel with him in fifteen minutes. Captain Gildrock may settle his case, though I fancy he will go for me the first chance he gets."

"He is sure to do that," added Bob Swanton.

"He may get a thrashing if he does," replied Dory.

"Don't be too sure of that, Dory. He is a fighting character, and has been turned out of three academies, to say nothing of half a dozen other schools. He rules the roost wherever he goes," continued Bob.

"He won't do it at Beech Hill," said Dory confidently.

"If he don't he will run away."

"He won't run a great ways before my uncle gets his paw upon him. I am going down to Burlington this afternoon, in the steamer, after my uncle. We shall pass the island, and he can do what he pleases with the fellow. I don't think I am any more afraid of him than he is of me."

During the rest of the passage the events we have narrated were fully discussed, and Dory learned more about the antecedents of Oscar Chester. Doubtless he was the worst fellow in the party; but, if the truth had been known, Dory would have understood that some of the others were not much better. In three hours from Burlington the Goldwing arrived at the little lake on which Beech Hill was located.

Mr. Brookbine, a very intelligent carpenter, who had been engaged as an instructor in this department, was on the wharf; and the new pupils were handed over to him. He marched them to the dormitory, where the boys deposited what little baggage they brought. The Sylph lay at the wharf, and the smoke was pouring out of her smoke-stack; for Jepson had received a telegraph-message from Captain Gildrock.

The boys were more interested in the steam-yatch than in any thing else; and they immediately asked permission of Mr. Brookbine, as they had before of Dory, to go to Burlington in her. The master-carpenter was willing; but he decided to go with them, after the experience which Dory had had with them on the passage up.

Dory was the pilot, and he took his place in the pilot-house. He was perfectly at home there; and the Sylph was really under his command, for the carpenter knew nothing about boats or navigation. In a discussion in regard to Oscar Chester, Mr. Brookbine thought he had better be taken on board, for it would be late before they returned from Burlington. A boat was sent for him, and he was brought on board.

CHAPTER XI.

THE MASTER-CARPENTER DISPOSES OF HIS PRISONER.

OSCAR CHESTER had been on Garden Island over two hours, and had had time enough to cool off. It was plain that he did not like the looks of Mr. Brookbine, who was a stalwart Vermonter, over six feet in height. He had gone on shore with one of the men from the estate, who acted as a deck-hand, to bring off the rebel.

Oscar said nothing when he went on board of the steamer, and the other boys were not inclined to make any talk with him. He walked from one end of the Sylph to the other, taking a hasty survey of the steam-yacht. He did not appear to be looking for any thing in particular.

When he was on the forward deck he discovered Dory in the pilot-house. He did not even bestow a second glance upon him, and went aft in a few minutes. He looked sullen and obstinate, and it was clear that he was disgusted with his experience on the lake.

"No use, Oscar," said Williston Orwell, as the rebel approached him at the stern of the boat. "You haven't made out any thing, and I don't believe you will."

"The end of the world hasn't come yet," replied Oscar with a heavy sneer. "There is time enough yet, and you know I never back down."

"But you might as well. You began too soon," added Will Orwell.

"I didn't begin at all: I was civil enough to Dory till he began to put on airs. He talked to me just as though I were a little child, and he were the Grand Mogul. I told him I wanted to steer the boat, and he told me to sit down. He insulted me."

"I don't think he did, Oscar. None of us were ever in a sailboat before; and I think he did just right in not letting you steer, for it wouldn't have taken much to upset that boat with so many in her."

"Then you think I am a spring chicken, do you, Will?" demanded Oscar with a curl of the lip.

"You know I don't think any such thing; but you don't know how to steer a sailboat any more than I do. You were a little too fast to think of doing it so soon," reasoned Orwell with proper deference, though he ventured to speak the truth as he understood it.

"If the fellow hadn't put on airs, and ordered me about as though I had been his servant, I wouldn't say a word," continued Oscar. "As it is, he insulted me, and pitched me into the lake."

"He didn't pitch you into the lake, Oscar. You are not used to a boat tossed about by the waves, and you fell overboard."

"Didn't he make the boat tip more when I stood up on purpose to pitch me into the lake?" demanded Oscar angrily.

"I don't know whether he did or not. I don't understand a boat."

"I know he did! And then he tumbled me into the water at the island."

"But you pitched into him then; and, as he could stand up better than you could in the boat, he threw you overboard."

"I shall get even with him; and if I don't throw him into the lake, it will be because I can't do it," blustered the rebel. "I see you are on his side."

"I am not on his side; but I don't expect a

fellow to stand still, and let you thrash him. I advise you to let him alone for a while, and your time will come before many days have gone by. Don't touch him while he is handling the boat," added the politic companion.

"I shall go for him the first moment I can get at him, and I know where he is now," said the intemperate rebel.

"Don't do it: Dory is the pilot of the steamer, and the engineer just told me that they can do nothing without him. Didn't you hear Captain Gildrock read the telegraph-message, that Dory was away, and for that reason he could not go down to Burlington to convey us to Beech Hill?" reasoned Will very earnestly.

"I don't care what he is: I shall not feel easy for a moment until I get even with him. I will pull him out of that cubby-house where he is, and pitch him into the lake, before I am half an hour older," persisted the rebel.

"Don't do it! You will only make trouble for yourself. Captain Gildrock will come on board as soon as we get to Burlington, and if I mistake not you will find a Tartar in him."

"I'm not afraid of him. But I don't think I

shall wait for him," replied Oscar. "I have not been to Beech Hill yet, but I have had about enough already to satisfy me what it is going to be. If I am to be ordered about by a boy younger than I am, and insulted by him, because I happen to be in a boat with him, I don't want any more of it. My uncle gave me money enough to pay my fare to New York, and you have more than I have, Will. What do you say: will you go with me?"

"What shall we do when we get there? I don't believe in jumping out of the frying-pan into the fire," replied Will.

"Both of us want to go to sea, and all we have to do is to find places in a ship going to some foreign country. We can take care of ourselves," said Oscar confidently.

"I am not ready to go anywhere yet: I want to see what this Industrial School is. We are to learn how to handle an engine, and how to manage ships and boats. I think we had better wait a while before we go to New York. We haven't money enough to pay our way till we find a place in a ship."

"You can do as you like, Will, but I have had enough of this thing; and when you miss me you will know where I have gone. If you blow on me "—

"You know very well I won't do that," protested Will.

Oscar did not wait to hear any more. He went forward, and then ascended to the hurricane deck. He and Will Orwell had been cronies, so far as the character of Oscar would permit such a relation.

The rebel reached the hurricane deck, and went forward to the pilot-house. He surveyed the situation carefully. Dory stood before an open window, with the spokes of the wheel in his hands. The doors of the apartment, one on each side, were open. The young helmsman had no more thought of being assaulted than he had of jumping overboard.

Dory was delighted with his occupation, for he had not steered the Sylph enough to make it an old story to him. From Garden Island he had run out into the lake until the steamer was in range between Split Rock and Juniper Island lights, when he headed for the latter. This course would carry him clear of Quaker Smith Reef.

Most of the boys, after looking over the Sylph

with wonder and astonishment at the elegance of her appointments, had gathered on the main deck forward, where they could see the lake and the course of the steamer. But a few of them were on the hurricane-deck, and three of them were in the pilot-house with Dory. The pilot kept his eye on Juniper Island lighthouse, the top of which could be seen seventeen miles. The flag-pole in the bow was kept in range with the object for which he was steering. He had just explained to the boys in the room how he kept off the rocks and shoals, and found his way to any part of the lake.

He had hardly finished this explanation before Oscar Chester rushed into the pilot-house. He rudely knocked aside a couple of the pilot's auditors, and laid violent hands upon Dory. The helmsman was unconscious of the presence of an enemy until the rebel had seized him by the collar of his coat. He pulled him over on his back upon the floor.

"Your time has come now, Dory Dornwood!" said Oscar fiercely, as he began to drag Dory out of the pilot-house.

"So has yours!" added Mr. Brookbine, as he

stepped forward from behind the pilot-house, where he had been reading the morning paper brought up by the Goldwing.

The master-carpenter took the rebel by the nape of the neck, and snapped him off his feet before he could wink twice. He pitched him half-way across the hurricane deck. Oscar was nothing but a "spring chicken" in the hands of the burly mechanic.

"It's a pity I took you off that island!" exclaimed Mr. Brookbine, as he bestowed a glance of contempt upon the rebel. "Did he hurt you, Dory?"

"Not at all. He came up behind me when I was not thinking of any thing of that kind, or I should have taken care of myself," replied the young pilot, as he rushed back to the wheel.

The pilot got his range again, and the Sylph went ahead as though nothing had happened. The master-carpenter walked up to the fallen rebel, who appeared to have been hurt when he struck the deck, though he was in the act of getting up. Mr. Brookbine did not wait for him to finish the act, but seized him by the nape of the neck again, and bore him to the pilot-house.

"It is a pity we took this fellow from the island, Dory, for we can't trust him loose about the steamer," said the stout Vermonter. "Is there any place on board where I can lock him up?"

"Put him in the ice-house," replied Dory, who was entirely willing to have his assailant placed where he could do no more mischief.

"Let me alone!" growled Oscar, attempting to break away from the grip of the master-carpenter.

"I will let you alone when I have locked you in the ice-house," added Mr. Brookbine, giving his patient several sharp twists and shakes, which certainly did not improve his temper.

"He sneaked up behind me, or I should not have needed any help," said Dory, who felt that he had suffered a partial defeat in being taken by surprise. "I am sorry I did not see him, for I think I should have made it hot for him."

"I shall make it hot for you before you have seen the end of this affair. I will teach you what it is to insult your betters," replied Oscar. "If I don't pitch you into the lake before I have done with you, it will be because I can't."

"Any time when you are ready, let the fun

begin," added Dory, when he had better have held his tongue.

"You will cool off in the ice-house; and we will see what you can do in there," continued Mr. Brookbine, as he dragged the rebel out of the pilot-house.

"Let me alone! I don't let anybody put his hands upon me," yelled Oscar, struggling to escape from the grasp of the carpenter.

"But you will be a good boy, and let me put my hands upon you, won't you?" added the big mechanic.

"No, I won't! I will be the death of you if you don't let go!"

"Steady, my boy: you are getting excited. You are wasting a great deal of bad breath on nothing."

The carpenter slapped his victim over a few times on the deck before he reached the stairs to the main deck. Oscar could not stand this: he said it hurt, and he became comparatively quiet. His tyrant walked him down the steps. The boys on both decks gathered to witness the exciting scene; but no one offered to interfere, and no one spoke a word of comfort for the rebel.

"Will Orwell!" called the victim, when he saw his crony among the spectators to his humiliation. "Come here, and help me!"

"No, I thank you! I don't believe in butting your head against a stonewall, and I told you not to do it beforehand."

The carpenter opened the door of the ice-house, and thrust his prisoner into the dark hole, as it was when the door was closed.

CHAPTER XII.

CAPTAIN GILDROCK'S FIRST LESSON IN NAVIGATION.

MR. BROOKBINE secured the door of the ice-house, and put the key into his pocket. The interior was ventilated for the benefit of the provisions that were kept on the ice when the steamer was on a long cruise, but there was no window or other opening which would admit a particle of light.

"What's the trouble, Mr. Brookbine?" asked Jepson the engineer, who was the master-machinist and an instructor of the school.

"That is the most desperate young cub I ever happened to encounter," replied the carpenter, as he proceeded to relate what had happened in the Goldwing and on board of the steamer.

"Captain Gildrock will bring him to his senses," added the engineer, laughing; for he believed the captain could do any thing that was within the scope of mortal man.

"I am ready to have him begin where I leave off; but there won't be much left of the young rascal when I get through with him if I have to deal with him," replied the carpenter.

"We are likely to have a sweet time with these young fellows if many of them are like that one," added Mr. Jepson. "He wants to get even with Dory, does he? I reckon Dory will be willing to give him a chance, though I never knew of the skipper's getting into a fight on his own account."

Dory had already become a great favorite at Beech Hill. He was a smart boy, but he was not perfect by any means. He had a great deal to learn, but he was willing to learn it. The instructors in the scholastic department had not yet arrived, but the mechanical directors were already his fast friends. Even the servants, of whom there was a small army on the estate, always smiled when he went among them; for he was invariably kind and obliging to them, and willing to assist them by all the means in his power. Besides, he was regarded as the heir of the magnate of Beech Hill; and it was prudent to "keep on the right side of him."

Of course the nine other boys who had arrived

that day all talked about the exciting events which had transpired since they left Burlington in the forenoon. Still, no one belonging to the steamer heard them say any thing. They made no comments on the conduct of Oscar: possibly they were afraid they might be reported to him. But they had learned to feel a great admiration for Dory; first, because he was not afraid of the rebel, and, second, because he could handle a sailboat and manage a steamer.

It was about dark when the Sylph arrived at the landing in Burlington. Captain Gildrock was on the wharf, waiting her coming. As soon as he went on board, Mr. Brookbine reported the case of discipline to him, and informed him that the prisoner was confined in the ice-house.

"All right: let him stay there," replied the captain, when he had listened to the account of the doings of the new scholar. "Then Dory has had a hard time of it. I was afraid he might have some difficulty."

"No fear for Dory," replied the carpenter, laughing. "He can take care of himself. He fought his own battle in the Goldwing, and won the day every time."

"I knew that Chester was the worst fellow in the party, but I did not expect him to break out so soon. I am glad to hear that the others have behaved well," said Captain Gildrock, as he walked forward where the boys were assembled. "How are you getting on, boys?"

"First-rate, sir," replied several of them in the same breath.

"I am glad to hear it; and none of us will have any trouble as long as we mean well. What you mean is more than half the battle in morals. I did not expect you so soon, and I am afraid Dory has not looked out for your stomachs."

"Yes, he has, sir," said Ben Ludlow. "He had a basket of provisions on the boat, and we fed out of that."

This was the lunch he had taken the night before, and it had served over a dozen instead of two. But the boys had been so much excited by the novel event of a sail in a fresh breeze that they were not in condition to do justice to the rations.

When the captain learned that the scholars had eaten only the supply of food intended for two, he took the whole party to the hotel to supper.

After Captain Gildrock and Dory returned, the engineer and carpenter went. The latter suggested that the prisoner in the ice-house had been forgotten.

"I shall not forget him, but he may go without his supper to-night. A little fasting will do him good. His father and mother are both dead, and his uncle is one of the richest men in the State. He told me that nothing but the sharpest discipline would do him any good. He will run away as soon as he gets a chance; and this must be prevented," replied the captain.

Jepson and Brookbine returned in less than half an hour. The captain had quite a chat with the boys while they were waiting. He told them something about his plans, and was so kind and familiar with them that they began to like him.

"I am told that some of you have been wild boys, and have been turned out of school," said he. "Except in one instance, I don't know who they are. I prevented your parents and others from telling me any thing about your misconduct. You are all alike to me so far, and every boy has his own reputation to make.

"You will not be judged at all by the past, but

by what you do in the future. I want you to remember this, boys. All of you will have to work in the shops, and wherever there is any thing to do. You will have to learn your book-lessons as well as how to work in wood and metal. But there will be lots of fun as well as hard work. In a few days we shall man this steamer, and every one of you will have a station on board of her."

"Hurrah!" shouted one of the new pupils in his enthusiasm; and the cheer was taken up by the entire party.

"Before winter I hope some of you will be as competent to handle a sailboat or a steamer as Dory is. But bear in mind that it is not all play. I am going to make useful men of you, and I hope you will second all my endeavors."

The arrival of the carpenter and engineer interrupted the conversation, and in a few minutes more the Sylph was standing up the lake. It was dark now; and the boys gathered around Captain Gildrock again, for he could not talk without interesting them.

"Who is steering this steamer now, Captain Gildrock?" asked Jim Alburgh.

"Dory is steering her," replied the captain.

"But it is dark: how can he find his way back to Beech Hill?"

"Did you suppose that ships that cross the ocean, being out of sight of land for weeks at a time, stopped in the night?" asked the captain.

"I didn't think any thing at all about it," replied Jim. "I don't know any thing about it. It is as dark as a pocket, and I should not think Dory could see the land on either side of the lake."

"He has no need to see it. Do you see that lighthouse on the island?" asked the captain, pointing at Juniper Island.

"But that does not give light enough to enable the pilot to see the shore on either side," replied Jim.

"That is not what a lighthouse is for. The light it gives don't amount to any thing half a mile from it. The light only marks certain localities. Now look up the lake all of you," continued Captain Gildrock, pointing in the direction of Split-Rock light. "Do you see that light?"

"Yes, sir!" shouted Lick Milton. His name was T. Licking Milton, but he had a nickname.

The rest of the boys soon made out the light, and some of them shouted as loudly as the first speaker.

"Juniper Island light is on our right now. Dory will run on till the steamer is in range with this light and Split Rock, which is twelve miles and a half from here. Then he will head for the Split-Rock light, keeping Juniper exactly astern of him," continued the captain.

"Why don't he run for Split Rock now?" asked Ben Ludlow.

"He would run upon Quaker-Smith's Reef, about four miles from here, if he did. Now, my boy, can you walk straight from where you stand to the flag-pole at the stem of the steamer?"

"No, sir, I cannot. That thing is in the way," replied Ben, after he had looked the matter over.

"Precisely so: the capstan is in your way. Now go over to the side of the steamer." Ben obeyed, and the boys watched the demonstration with interest. "Can you walk straight to the stem of the boat now?"

"Yes, sir, I can. There is nothing in my way."

"Then, if you keep in range with the port gangway and the stem, there will be nothing in your way, will there?"

"Nothing, sir."

"That is exactly the principle on which we

pilot a steamer or any other vessel. But sometimes the matter is much more complicated, and we have to take a dozen different ranges in going a dozen miles. Pilots learn all these ranges, and get their bearings from various objects on the shore. You can see the capstan; but we cannot see the obstructions in our way in sailing a vessel, for they are under water. They are all laid down on the chart, and we can learn our courses from that."

"But isn't there any thing on that reef to let you know where it is?" asked Dave Windsor.

"There is nothing on Quaker-Smith's Reef, for it is out of the usual track of vessels. It is about a mile from the eastern shore of the lake. When the water is as low as it is now, this steamer would get aground on it. But at the entrance to harbors they put buoys, and also on rocks and shoal places in or near the usual track of vessels."

"What sort of things are buoys?" asked Bob Swanton.

"Generally they are logs of wood, anchored to the bottom. These are called spar-buoys. Others are made of metal, hollow, and shaped like a couple of frustrums of cones joined at the big end.

These are can-buoys. There are other kinds, but you won't find them in this lake."

"Spar and can buoys. We can remember them," added John Brattle.

"The spars are all painted red, black, or striped. When going into a harbor, red buoys must be left on the starboard hand; that is, on your right. Black buoys must be left on the port, or left, hand. When you see a buoy painted with black and red stripes, it is a danger buoy; and you may go on either side of it. When you see one painted up and down with black and white stripes, you must go close to it. Sometimes the buoys are numbered: then the even numbers are on the red buoys, and the odd ones on the black buoys. But you must learn all these things by seeing them."

"What are the colored lights on the sides of this steamer for?" asked Bob Swanton.

"The red light is on the port side, and the green on the starboard. They are to show any vessel approaching us which way we are going," replied the captain. "But I can explain this better when we see the lights of another vessel."

All hands were on the lookout for another vessel at once.

CHAPTER XIII.

HANDLING A STEAMER IN A FOG.

HALF an hour later a steamer came out of Essex, on the west shore of the lake. Captain Gildrock was promptly notified by the boys that a red light was to be seen.

"I suppose you have all seen port wine, and know it is red; though it is not as red in Portugal as it is here," added the captain. "This will help you to remember that the red light is on the port, or left-hand, side. When I see the red, I know at once that the port side of the vessel is towards me, and therefore, if I am to the northward of her, that she is going in an easterly direction. If I were south of her, she would be going the other way."

"But now we can see the green light too," said Dave Windsor.

"That shows that she is coming towards us, and we must look out that she don't run into us."

"How can you help it, if she keeps on, and you keep on?" asked Ned Bellows.

"We will wait and see what Dory will do," replied Captain Gildrock.

After going a mile farther, the boys heard a single sharp whistle over their heads. It was immediately followed by the same signal from the approaching steamer.

"That will make it all right. Dory has blown one whistle, which means that he will pass the other steamer to starboard. The other steamer, as she indicates by her one whistle, will pass at the starboard of us," continued the captain. "If Dory had blown two whistles, he would have gone to port of the approaching vessel. You see that we are going by her all right."

"Suppose there had been a fog when we came out of Burlington, Captain Gildrock: what should we have done?" asked Ben Ludlow. "Could Dory have run the boat down to Beech Hill?"

"He could do it, but I should rather he would not. It is not safe to run in a fog; and it is best not to do it, unless your business is very urgent," replied Captain Gildrock.

"But suppose you could not even see Juniper-Island light: what would you do if you had to run to Beech Hill?" persisted the inquirer.

"Juniper light is west-south-west from the wharf, as I have ruled it off from the chart. The distance is three and a quarter miles. The speed of the Sylph is twelve miles an hour, and it will take her sixteen minutes and a quarter to reach the light. But we don't start at full speed, and we must allow for that.

"At the end of sixteen minutes, by the clock in the pilot-house, we begin to look out for the light. If we don't find it, we don't go ahead, if we stay there all day and all night. We whistle, and that lets the people at the light know that a steamer is trying to find her way up the lake; and they will blow a horn. When we hear it, we know by the direction where the light is. They will keep blowing the horn for a while.

"Split-Rock light is south-south-west from Juniper, and we steer this course by compass for one hour and two minutes. At the end of that time, if we are all right, we hear the horn at Split Rock. When we have got the bearing of the light, we head her south by west, and run two and three-quarters miles to the mouth of Beaver River; which we do in thirteen and three-quarters minutes.

"Then Dory will strike the bell for the deck-hand to heave the lead, or, in other words, see how deep the water is. If we get ten feet at this stage of the water, we are in the channel. We steer east-south-east, and keep sounding all the time. If the leadsman should report a less depth, we stop the steamer, and find where the channel is. We may have to get out a boat to ascertain. When we get fairly into the river, we can see the shores through the fog. If we can't, we have to feel our way up."

The evening was quite chilly on the lake; and Captain Gildrock had taken the boys into the forward cabin, as they were not provided with overcoats. He had hardly finished his explanation before a long whistle above them excited their interest.

"Perhaps you will have a chance to see how we work the steamer in a fog," said Captain Gildrock, looking at his watch. "It is about time we were up with Split Rock, and very likely Dory cannot find the light."

The captain left the cabin, followed by all the boys. As soon as they reached the forecastle, Dory rang the bell to stop her. The fog had blown up from the southward; and the Sylph was completely enveloped in it, so that nothing could be seen from her deck.

"Here we are," said Captain Gildrock, as he led the way to the hurricane-deck. "You can't see half a ship's-length ahead. I was afraid this southerly wind might blow up a fog."

The deck-hand was standing on the rail at the forward flag-pole, trying to penetrate the thick mist that shrouded the shore. Dory gave another long whistle. By this time the steamer had come to a standstill, and nothing more was to be done until the pilot found out where he was. The boys gathered on the hurricane-deck around Captain Gildrock, who did not say any thing to the young pilot, or even go near him.

"Can you see any thing, Bates?" called Dory to the deck-hand.

"Not a thing, sir," replied Bates.

"There! I hear the horn!" exclaimed Dave Windsor.

"Horn on the starboard bow, sir!" shouted Bates.

"I hear it," added Dory. The gong-bell in the engine-room rang, and the Sylph began to move again.

"Horn again, sir. We are not ten fathoms from the point, sir," called Bates. "I see the light now, sir."

"All right: so do I. Keep a sharp lookout ahead, Bates," replied Dory, as the sound of a jingling bell was heard from the engine-room; and the steamer increased her speed very rapidly.

"Bates seems to be a very polite man," said Ned Bellows, laughing. "He puts in a 'sir' every time he says any thing to Dory."

"It is second nature for a seaman to say 'sir' to an officer," added the captain.

"But to a boy not more than fourteen or fifteen years old!"

"No matter how young or how old he is, if he is an officer. Discipline is very strict at sea, as it will be on board of the Sylph after we have organized the ship's company. You must all say 'sir' to your officers, even if they are boys."

"The last bell that rung was different from the other," suggested Ben Ludlow.

"The jingling bell is the speed-bell," replied the captain.

"It means 'Go faster,' don't it?"

"Not at all. If Dory should ring it now, it would mean 'Go slower.'"

"It can't mean both slower and faster," reasoned Ben.

"Why not? If the boat is going full speed it means 'Slow down:' if she is going at half speed it means 'Full speed.' The gong-bell, one stroke, means 'Start her' if she is not turning her screw, or 'Stop her' if she is going ahead. Two strokes of the gong means 'Back her.'"

At equal intervals the whistle of the Sylph sounded, and this fact soon excited the attention of the curious pupils. They wanted to know what it was for. The captain explained that it was to warn any vessel of the presence of the steamer, so that neither craft should run into the other. Steamers used their whistles, and sailing-vessels a horn. But no horn or whistle was heard during the rest of the trip.

The next sound that attracted the attention of the pupils was the speed-bell, which was quickly followed by the gong; and the screw ceased to turn. At a single stroke of the large ship's bell, Bates, standing upon the rail, at the forward gangway, heaved the lead.

"No bottom!" shouted the leadsman. Dory rang the gong, and the steamer went ahead at half speed.

"Does he mean to say there is no bottom to the lake in this place, Captain Gildrock?" asked Dave Windsor.

"Not at all: we don't usually sound below fifty feet; and any greater depth than that is called 'no bottom,'" replied the captain.

"By the deep, eight!" said Bates.

"By the deep, eight," repeated Dave Windsor. "That means eight feet deep, I suppose."

"No, it don't: it means about forty-eight feet. The depth is measured in fathoms of six feet each. The lead-line is marked with two strips of leather at two fathoms, with three strips at three, with a white rag at five fathoms, and with a red rag at seven; at ten fathoms is a leather with a hole in it, and so on. There are no marks at four, six, eight, and nine fathoms. When the leadsman said 'By the deep, eight,' the line was under water about six feet below the red rag, or seven fathoms."

"By the mark, five!" called Bates.

"Just thirty feet," the captain explained.

"And a half two!"

"Two fathoms and a half. We are shoaling rapidly."

"Mark under water, two!"

"A little over two fathoms."

"Ten feet!" shouted Bates with more energy than before.

The gong rang at this report, and two strokes followed instantly. The screw began to turn backwards; and, when her headway was checked, a single stroke stopped her.

"Dory is doing it all right," said Captain Gildrock. "When he backed her he put the helm to port, so as to get her head pointed east-south-east. If he had not stopped the boat when he did, she would have been aground in a couple of minutes; for there is a shoal south of the mouth of the river on which the water is only from one to six feet deep."

"What harm would it have done if we had got aground?" asked Bob Swanton.

"It would have done no harm, as we were going slowly; though we might have had to stay here all night. If there had been a rock there, it would probably have stove a hole in the bottom of the boat."

"Ten feet!" reported Bates again.

The gong rang to go ahead, but the steamer

hardly moved through the water. The captain said the pilot had told the engineer, through the speaking-tube, to go very slowly. Bates continued to sound, reporting the same water as before.

"I see the point, sir," said Bates a little later.

"All right! I have it," replied Dory. The boat began to move a little faster, but she did not get above half speed.

In the river the fog was not so dense as on the lake, and the pilot could make out the objects on the banks of the stream. She went into the creek leading from the river to the lake, and in a few minutes more she was at the temporary wharf which had been built for her.

"Well, boys, you have had both the theory and the practice of handling a steamer in a fog. It is an easy matter on this lake compared with the bays and harbors on the seacoast, for there the pilot has to make allowances for the tide."

The boys landed, and were directed to go to the study-room in a building adjoining the dormitory. The captain called Mr. Brookbine, and they went together to the ice-house.

CHAPTER XIV.

THE STRONG-ROOM AT THE BEECH-HILL INDUSTRIAL SCHOOL.

THE trip was finished, and Dory was relieved from further duty in the pilot-house. He came down upon the main deck just as the carpenter was unlocking the door of Oscar Chester's prison. Mr. Brookbine had a lantern in one hand, which threw its light into the room when the door was opened.

The rebel was lying on the floor, which was quite dry, for the room had not been used for several weeks. He seemed to be making himself quite at home in his prison; and possibly he had been asleep, for he gaped and yawned when he was discovered. But this was affectation. He wanted to make his persecutors, as he regarded them, think that he was not at all disturbed by his confinement.

"You may came out now, Chester," said Captain Gildrock.

"I don't want to go out: I am very comfortable here, I want you to understand," replied Oscar with plentiful display of bravado.

"It is my order that you come out!" added the captain sternly.

"I don't know that I care for your orders. I have made up my mind to stay in this place only long enough to get even with that Dory Dornwood. When I have thrashed him within an inch of his life, I shall be ready to leave; and I shall leave, I want you to understand," answered Oscar. "I don't intend to be bossed by any little boy you may see fit to place over me."

"I shall not argue the question with you: I told you to come out," continued Captain Gildrock in very decided, though gentle, tones.

"And I told you I wouldn't go out!" replied Oscar.

"You may bring him out, Mr. Brookbine, and take him up to the brig," said the captain, as he took the lantern from the hand of the carpenter.

"You have brought that big bully, have you?" demanded the rebel, rising from his reclining position.

No one replied to this demand, but the carpenter walked into the prison. Oscar was disposed to show fight. He retreated to a corner, and put himself in the attitude of defence. Suddenly, as if by impulse, the prisoner began to feel in his pockets; but the stout mechanic did not give him time enough to produce any thing. He took him by the collar of his coat, and lifted him off the floor. With his other hand, he jerked the hands of the prisoner out of his pockets. As he did so, a two-bladed knife dropped from one of them.

Possibly the sight of this article kindled the anger of the carpenter, for he began to bang the captive about in a manner that threatened serious bodily injury to the victim.

"Hold on to him, but don't hurt him any more than may be necessary," interposed Captain Gildrock. "We can cure him of his infirmity in a few days."

"The rascal wants to knife me, and I am inclined to shake the bad blood out of him," replied the mechanic.

"He is a lunatic: he is boiling over with bad passions. A few days in the brig will cool him off. We will treat him as a sick boy; and, when he gets better, we will talk with him. Possibly there may be some reason in him when he is himself, if he ever is himself. If we can't manage him, we will send him to the lunatic-asylum," said the captain, as the carpenter dragged his prisoner out upon the deck.

Dory picked up the knife, and followed his uncle to the school-buildings in the rear of the mansion. Oscar could not stand the discipline of the burly Vermonter. He soon found, if he had not learned it before, that he was powerless in the hands of his persecutor; and he walked quietly in the direction he was led.

Captain Gildrock had expected to have some just such boys as Oscar Chester. In fact, he knew of this very one; for his uncle had applied to him to take him, as soon as he knew that he intended to open a mechanical institution. Mr. Chester was an old friend of the captain, to whom the latter had described his educational plan. This was the reason he happened to know all about Oscar, while he had taken pains not to be informed in regard to the antecedents of all his other pupils.

The founder of the new school understood men and boys thoroughly. Some of his scholars must inevitably be rebellious and troublesome, and he had fully provided for the treatment of such cases. He had erected two temporary buildings, one of which was the dormitory and the other the workshop and schoolroom, the latter occupying the story over the former. The students were to take their meals in the large dining-room of the mansion.

The dormitory consisted of twenty-four sleeping-rooms, each of which had been furnished with an iron bedstead and such simple furniture as might be required. Nothing was extravagant, or even elegant; for the school was an experiment which might succeed or fail.

In a small brick building close to the shop, a steam-engine had already been set up, from which a belt extending into the shop was to run the lathes, circular-saws, planers, boring-machines, and other machinery. One part of the shop was for woodwork, and the other for iron. But most of the tools and apparatus had not yet been put in their places.

At one end of the dormitory was the "brig." Captain Gildrock's earliest experience at sea had been in the navy, where he had obtained his first ideas of discipline. The ship's prison on board a man-of-war is called the "brig." The captain had already given this name to his place of discipline.

It was one of the rooms of the dormitory, fitted up for the purpose intended. The walls and ceiling, as well as the floor, had been constructed of thick spruce plank. All the wood had been covered with sheet-iron. The two windows were grated with iron bars. It contained a narrow iron bedstead, an iron stand for a table, and one chair of the same material. The locks on the door were strong enough for any prison. But not even the door could be seen from the hall of the dormitory, for it was concealed by a wooden partition in front of it.

No boy was to be allowed to visit this strong-room unless he was condemned to become an occupant of it for his misconduct. He had not mentioned it to the boys, and the instructors were requested not to do so. The iron in the room was all painted black, so that it was an exceedingly gloomy-looking apartment. The captain hoped he should never have occasion to make any use of the brig; and certainly he had not expected to have an occupant for it on the day the first of the boys arrived.

Mr. Brookbine took his prisoner to the brig, attended by the captain. He was hurried up the stairs, and thrust into the prison, without any ceremony. The lantern lighted up the gloomy den when the door was opened; and, if Oscar did not shrink from his fate, he had more nerve than ninety-nine in a hundred boys.

He did give a start when he looked into the brig, and it required some effort on the part of the mechanic to force him into it. In the dungeon he looked about him with something like an expression of disgust on his face. Then he seemed to feel that he was yielding somewhat to the circumstances; and he straightened up, and made an effort to "stiffen his back." His persecutors were retiring from the entrance, and the captain was about to close the door.

"I have eaten nothing since I had my breakfast, early this morning," said Oscar stiffly, when he saw that he was about to be locked into the cell for the night.

"It is your own fault. All the rest of the boys had supper at the hotel in Burlington," replied the captain.

"Do you mean to starve me?" demanded the prisoner.

"No, I don't mean to starve you. — Dory," called the captain at the open window in the hall: "go into the house and get a loaf of bread, a case-knife, and a pitcher of water."

In a few minutes the skipper of the Goldwing returned with the articles named, and Captain Gildrock placed them on the iron table.

"Am I to be fed on dry bread?" asked Oscar, as he looked with contempt upon the provision on the table.

"I don't answer questions at the present time. There is food: you can eat it or let it alone. You can stay in this place a day, a week, a month, or a year: the time depends upon yourself," said the captain, as he withdrew from the brig.

He closed the door, and secured it with the great lock. He also fastened the door in the plank partition, so that no student could get within six feet of the strong-room.

"That fellow will think better of it in a few days, perhaps by to-morrow," said Captain Gildrock, as they left the dormitory.

"For a boy, he is the hardest customer I ever

had to deal with," replied Brookbine. "There is no more reason in him than there is in a brickbat."

The captain led the way to the schoolroom, where the boys had assembled. They were behaving themselves very well, and they all applauded when the captain entered the room.

"Boys, there is nothing more to be done to-night. To-morrow will be Saturday; and we shall organize the ship's company for the Sylph, and take a little trip in her down the lake, perhaps as far as Plattsburgh. Your rooms are all ready for you, and you can retire as soon as possible. We have breakfast at seven in the morning."

The captain stood upon the platform, and made this little speech, which was applauded by the students. Mr. Brookbine was left to look after the pupils, and the captain and Dory went into the house. Though it was after nine o'clock in the evening, they found Mr. Bolingbroke Millweed and his mother in the sitting-room. Her son had related to her his adventures on the lake and in Burlington. She was very grateful to Dory for what he had done, and expressed herself to that effect in very high-flown speech.

"My son Bolingbroke informs me that you have manifested some interest in his future welfare, for which I am extremely grateful to you, Captain Gildrock. I hope you will be able to do something for him; for a word from you would secure for him a good place in a store," said Mrs. Millweed, after she had succeeded in introducing the subject.

"I offered your son a place in my school for a year. If he is going to accept the offer I made him, I want him here at seven to-morrow morning," replied the captain bruskly. "I don't know any thing about him, and I can't recommend him for a place in a store."

"I don't wish to make a mechanic of him," protested Mrs. Millweed. "I am looking for something higher than that for him."

"Do you think that being a counter-jumper is something higher?" demanded the captain, laughing heartily at the idea.

"I wish him to be a merchant; and I am sure that is higher and more respectable than a greasy mechanic," added the lady with a sneer.

"Very well, madam: I cannot do any thing for your son," added the captain decidedly. "There are ten times as many clerks as can find places now."

"I have never allowed my boys to work on the farm; and they haven't acquired any low ideas," continued Mrs. Millweed as she moved to the door, closely attended by Bolingbroke.

The visitors departed, and it was not probable that they would again darken the captain's door.

CHAPTER XV.

SOMETHING ABOUT THE AFFAIRS OF THE MILL-
WEED FAMILY.

LONG before breakfast-time the new boys were roaming about the estate, with Dory as their guide. He showed them the place, and treated them as handsomely as he knew how. They were not in a boat, with a fresh wind blowing; and he had no occasion to use a single sharp word, and he had not on board of the Goldwing, except to Oscar Chester. By this time he had become quite popular with the students.

"Dory," called Captain Gildrock, as the skipper and his party came to the shop: "what was the name of the man that stole the money at the store?"

"Tim Lingerwell: he was the head man of Mr. Longbrook," replied Dory. "He came from this place."

"I know all about him," said a stranger who had been talking with the captain. "He never was any too good to do such a thing; and my son was lucky to get out of the scrape as well as he did."

This man was the father of Bolingbroke Millweed. For the first time he had heard about the Beech-Hill Industrial School that morning. His wife had told him about the captain's offer to take Bolingbroke into the school. He had been telling the shipmaster his troubles, and he wanted his son to accept the offer.

"I am a peaceable man, Captain Gildrock, and my wife has always had her own way," continued Farmer Millweed. "I don't like to have any trouble in the family, but I have gone just about as far as I can go."

The early visitor looked very sad, and choked a little, as though a few tears would relieve him. He stood looking upon the ground, trying to check his emotions.

"Things have gone hard with you, have they?" said Captain Gildrock in a sympathizing tone.

"Very hard, captain; and I don't know what is going to become of me and my family. I expect we shall fetch up in the poorhouse; as we certainly shall if things keep on as they have been," replied the farmer with a suppressed groan.

"I am sorry for you," added the captain. "I will take your son, and he shall be of no expense to you for a year; and at the end of that time, I will guarantee that he will be able to do something for you, and take care of himself besides."

"Just as soon as I heard of your offer, I came right over here; for I want to have Bolly learn a trade," said the farmer. "He will be provided for, whatever becomes of the rest of us. When my oldest girl was a dozen years old, I owned my farm free and clear; and I didn't owe any man on earth a single cent. Now there is a mortgage of two thousand dollars on my place, and I owe over a thousand dollars besides."

"You have been making bad speculations then," suggested Captain Gildrock.

"I never went into a speculation of any kind, captain; and I never lost any money in any way. Ten years ago I used to get a good living off my farm. We had plenty to eat, drink, and to wear. Now we don't have any thing." And, in spite of his struggles to restrain them, a flood of tears poured down his wan cheek.

"If you have had no misfortunes, I don't understand why things have gone so badly with you. But it is best to look into the matter, and find out what the trouble is, so that you can correct the errors of the past. You are not a very old man, and you may get out of the trouble yet."

"I know what the difficulty is well enough; and I have known it for two or three years, if not for ten. I have to take care of my family, consisting of my wife, two sons, and two daughters. The oldest is twenty-two, and the youngest is sixteen. My wife has high notions for a farmer's wife, and I have given in to her. She would not let the boys work on the farm; and, when I wanted any help, I had to hire. I suppose the girls helped their mother, but all of them had to dress like ladies. And that is where all the money I could get went to," said Millweed bitterly.

"The first thing is to stop the leak," suggested the captain in nautical terms. "If you don't stop it, the ship will go to the bottom."

"I know that very well, but I don't see how I'm going to stop the leak. All the children had to go to the high-school, and dress as smartly as the sons and daughters of rich men; though it was more than I could do to get the money to pay for it."

"But couldn't your wife see how things were going?" asked the captain.

"I talked with her, and told her seven years ago that I was running behindhand. I have talked with her twenty times since, and told her we should all fetch up in the poorhouse if we kept on. She said the boys would soon find places in stores, and help me. The girls could have had plenty of work at good wages, but their notions were as high as their mother's."

"I see how it is," said Captain Gildrock, nodding his head, as much as to declare that it was the old story.

"The girls are too proud to marry a farmer or a mechanic, and rich men's sons don't seem to want them. They are good girls enough, but they have got high notions. The boys never did do any thing, and I don't know whether they can or not. I want Bolly to try. Pemberton is eighteen, and I suppose he is too old for your new school."

"Not at all: I will take them both, but they will have to work."

"That's what they need. If I could get the boys into your school, I should like it first-rate, and I should have some hopes that I might get along; though I have got to lose my farm, and it won't fetch any thing over the mortgage," added the farmer very gloomily.

"I will take the two boys into my school; and, if the girls will go to work, I will find places for them in a store or factory."

"You are very kind, Captain Gildrock; but I am afraid my wife won't allow the boys to go to your school, or the girls to do any thing to help support themselves," added Farmer Millweed.

"I shall not meddle with the affairs of your family; but, if it was my case, I should set the boys and girls to work," added Captain Gildrock. "You must take the helm in your own hands."

"It will make trouble," said Farmer Millweed, shaking his head.

"You are very sure to have trouble if you don't do it."

"That's so!" exclaimed the unhappy man. "I have always had to work hard, and I never drank a drop of liquor in my life. I'm not as smart as some, but I've done my best to get along. Next month the mortgage and interest are due, and I have not a dollar to pay either. I am behindhand on my interest now. Of course Stubbs will take possession, and my family will be turned out of the house. I have no place to go, and the best I can do will be to go to work on wages; for all I have got will not pay my debts. I shall have to take the helm, as you call it, captain."

"If I can do any thing for you, I shall be glad to do it," added the captain.

"I haven't any claims on you, Captain Gildrock, and it is very kind of you to offer to take my boys. I will go home, and see what can be done," replied Farmer Millweed, as he left the captain.

There was an expression of resolution on his face as he passed out of the yard, and it was evident to the captain that he meant to do something in the emergency. The captain wondered if his pluck would hold out long enough to enable him to do it.

"If the boys are going to join the school, I want them here by nine this forenoon; for we are about to organize a ship's company for the steam-yacht," he called to the discouraged farmer, as he was passing through the gate.

"I intend to have them both here," answered Mr. Millweed.

"If they come, I shall do them more good than the high-school ever did," said the captain to himself, as he went into the house.

The captain insisted, at the breakfast-table, that the high-school had spoiled the Millweed boys and girls. Mr. Brookbine dissented, and was sure it was the mother who had made the mischief.

"It was she who sent them to the high-school; and the matter is about as broad as it is long," added the captain.

"But the mother could have spoiled them just as fully if they had not gone to the high-school," persisted the master-carpenter, who had opinions of his own. "I believe the high-school is a good thing; and, if these boys and girls had gone to work when they got through, it would have been all right with the family. It was the high notions, and not the high-school, that did the mischief; and the children got them from the mother. The father is a man of no great force."

"But he had force enough to take care of his family, and lay up something, until he was broken down by the demands of his family upon him. There was a screw loose somewhere, and the children ought never to have gone to the high-school."

"Perhaps not: I think myself that the high-school business is sometimes overdone," replied the mechanic. "I never went to a high-school or an academy, but I don't think I should have been any the worse off for a great deal more learning than I ever got."

"I am willing to admit that the high-school is a necessity in an American community, but I think it ought to be combined with something of an industrial character. The occupation of the mechanic should be redeemed from the odium which has attached to it."

"I agree with you there," added Mr. Brookbine heartily. "The Millweed boys must have been good scholars to get through when they were only sixteen. Most of the scholars that graduate are eighteen and nineteen."

"And those who are not going into the learned professions have wasted three years which ought to have been spent in the shop, or in learning the business of life. The graduates come out, a year or two before they are of age, with too high notions to do any thing but measure tape; and that they call being merchants."

Captain Gildrock was very radical in his notions, and he continued the conversation until the meal was over. The boys were directed to take their overcoats, and go on board of the Sylph.

"The prisoner in the brig wants to see you, Captain Gildrock," said Mr. Brookbine, just as the captain was going on board of the steamer.

"He must be attended to at once, for he needs more care than all the others," replied the captain, as he went back to the dormitory with the carpenter.

The mechanic unlocked the doors, and the captain presented himself before the rebel. Oscar looked very pale, and his chest heaved with emotion. It was evident, from the appearance of his eyes, that he had not slept well in his new quarters. A small portion of the bread on the table had been eaten, but not enough to indicate that he had been very hungry.

"I am told that you wish to see me," said the captain.

"I don't care to stay any longer in this place;

and I should like to have you send me back to my uncle," replied Oscar.

"If that is all you want, nothing more need be said. You will not be sent back to your uncle under any circumstances."

"Then I will do the best I can if you will let me out," added the rebel.

Oscar was promptly released without a question.

CHAPTER XVI.

THE ORGANIZATION OF THE SHIP'S COMPANY.

OSCAR CHESTER was taken to the house, and provided with a good breakfast. His appetite was not spoiled, though dry bread had no attractions for him. He ate heartily, and then walked down to the landing on the lake where the steamer lay.

Captain Gildrock had gone down before. He had called the boys together on the forward deck, where, as usual, they had greeted him with a cheer, which assured him so far that every thing was satisfactory to the pupils.

"Hereafter, my lads, I think we had better dispense with the cheers, except on extraordinary occasions. By and by something will occur that will not meet your approbation; and then you will want to make a demonstration of another kind," said the captain.

"Can't we make it?" asked Ben Ludlow.

"If what I do, and what the instructors do, is

not right, I should like to have you express your opinions in a proper manner," replied the principal of the school. "But, if any thing don't suit you, I don't wish you to manifest your disapprobation by hissing. Don't pretend to like what you don't like. Don't be hypocrites. But, if you are dissatisfied with any thing about the school, come to me, and express your minds in a proper manner; and we will calmly discuss the matter. If I am wrong, I shall make haste to set myself right; and I hope you will do the same."

This remark was greeted with a rousing cheer, for the boys were delighted with the discipline so far.

"I thought we were to dispense with the cheering," said the captain with a pleasant smile.

"That was an extraordinary occasion, Captain Gildrock," added Bob Swanton. "We never heard of a schoolmaster before who believed it possible for anybody to be right but himself."

The boys laughed and clapped their hands at this reply, and were ready to give Bob Swanton a medal for hitting the nail on the head at the right moment.

"The instructors here will try to be in the right.

If they don't, they won't be here long. But you and I may not always be able to agree, and I may have to insist on my own way. Then you must submit. But here comes Chester. I wish you all to refrain from saying any thing about what happened yesterday to him. We will all treat him handsomely, and it will be his own fault if he don't get along without any trouble."

Oscar came on board with the carpenter. He seemed to be much agitated, and probably he expected some sort of a greeting from his fellow-pupils. As they were not to say any thing to him about the past, they avoided even glancing at him, lest he might put a wrong construction upon their looks. Captain Gildrock appeared not to see him, and he took his place in the rear of the other boys. Possibly he was astonished to find that he had become a person of so little consequence.

"Now, my lads, we are to organize the ship's company," said the captain.

"Is this a ship?" asked Dave Windsor.

"This is simply a steamer; properly, a steam-yacht, being used mainly as a pleasure-craft. She is not a ship; but it is customary to speak of the ship's company, whatever the size or rig of the vessel. You read in the New Testament, speaking of Jesus, that he 'entered into a ship.' Have you an idea that the craft was a vessel with three masts, square rigged?"

"I did not know any thing about it," replied Will Orwell.

"That ship was nothing but a boat, not as big as the Goldwing probably. I repeat, that we are to organize the ship's company; and I assure you that the expression is quite correct."

"Of course it is," added Dave Windsor. "I only wanted to know about it."

"That's right: ask all the sensible things you can think of, and I shall be glad to answer you. You can't all be captains or even officers."

"We don't expect to be," added Ben Ludlow, when the captain paused to note the effect of his statement.

"It is necessary to have some privates on board; but one position is just as honorable as another if it is well filled," continued the captain. "There is to be no favoritism on board or in the school. Now, we must have firemen, deck-hands, cooks, and waiters; and it is just as important for you to learn the duties of these positions as those of officers."

"Are we to learn to cook?" asked Jim Alburgh, laughing.

"You are; and I consider this one of the most important parts to learn. I served as cook on board of a brig during one voyage to the West Indies; and I took as much pride in performing my duties correctly, as ever I did when commanding an East Indiaman," replied the principal with energy.

"I know something about cooking, and I like the business," added Jim Alburgh.

"Ah, here comes two recruits!" exclaimed Captain Gildrock, as Pemberton and Bolingbroke Millweed came on board. "I am particularly glad to see you, boys."

"Thank you, sir," replied Pemberton politely; and the principal was delighted to see that there was no appearance of compulsion in their coming.

"We have twenty-two of the pupils I want: four of them will join us at Burlington, and two more at Plattsburgh. I hope the other two will arrive before we begin the school."

"Are we going to Plattsburgh to-day, sir?" asked Bob Swanton.

"We are; and it is time we were moving,

though we have considerable to do before we can leave. I have concluded to be captain myself for the present, until I find a pupil who is competent to fill the place."

"Dory!" exclaimed several of the boys.

"Dory will not be captain, though I think he is competent. I want him in another place. He is my nephew, but he shall not be favored on that account. I have places for the twenty-four pupils of the school, and I will name them to you. Next to the captain will be the first and second officers, sometimes called mates, and, in men-of-war, lieutenants."

"But none of our crowd know any thing about steamers or boats, and are not fit for officers."

"The officers will learn their duties; and after a while, when you have all had a chance to know what is required of you, these positions will be given to those who are the most competent to fill them. The next in rank will be the first and second pilot. As Dory is the only one of you who is fitted to pilot a steamer, I shall appoint him first pilot. This is the only one I shall select for any place. All the others will be drawn by lot as soon as we leave Burlington."

A few of the pupils were disposed to applaud the appointment; but others hushed them up, and there was no demonstration.

"The third in rank are the engineers. As I am captain, Mr. Jepson will be the chief-engineer. We shall have a first and second assistant-engineer. Next come the first and second cook. Following this department is the steward's. The first, or chief, steward, the second, third, and fourth stewards, are the names of the places. Then come the firemen, of whom there will be four, and lastly the crew, or deck-hands as they are sometimes called. When we have twenty-four scholars, there will be eight of them."

The boys then asked a score of questions, which the captain answered with great good-nature, though some of them were trivial.

"Now, my lads, you wear the clothes in which you came from your homes. I have provided uniforms for you, which you will put on before we get under way."

Mr. Sheers, a tailor from the town, was in attendance to assist the boys in fitting themselves to the uniforms. This dress consisted of woollen shirts, blue sailor-pants, and short jackets. A

ORGANIZATION OF THE SHIP'S COMPANY.

white cap was given to each, and in half an hour all hands were on deck in their new rig. They looked very salt for a fresh-water lake, but the uniform was very neat and appropriate.

While the captain was talking to the pupils, Bates had brought on board a quantity of provisions and stores, which he had put in their proper places. The ice-house had received a supply, and every thing was ready for a start. Dory was directed to get under way, and he went to the pilot-house. Bates was on duty, and cast off the fasts when the signal was given. The bells rang, and the Sylph was soon moving out of the lake. In an hour and forty minutes she touched the wharf at Burlington. The Goldwing Club were on the pier, as they had been notified to be by Dory. Additional provisions were taken on board, and again the steamer was under way.

Captain Gildrock called all the students to the hurricane deck, where Dory could see what was going on. The boys were greatly excited, for they were curious to know what positions they would obtain. Captain Gildrock produced a number of white cards, and then stood up before the scholars. Taking a box which Bates brought to him, he dropped the cards into it, and then shook them up.

"Now, my lads, you will soon know who is cook and who is first officer," said the captain, as he placed the box on the shelf in the pilot-house, where the boys could reach it through one of the windows. "On each of the cards is written one of the positions of which I spoke to you. You will walk up to this window, reach into the box, and draw out one of the cards. You will not look into the box."

The captain drew the curtain over the window, so that it was impossible for any boy to see the interior of the box, as he had to thrust his arm through the folds of the curtain.

"If there is any thing unfair about this method of assigning the places, I want you to say so now," added the captain, when the preparations were completed.

"It is all as fair as any thing can be," added Dave Windsor; and all the others expressed their satisfaction.

"As fast as you draw your cards you will go down to the main deck. As you take the card from the box, you will give me your name; and I shall write it down in a book I have prepared for the purpose, against the name of the position. Now, one at a time."

Bob Swanton was the first to come forward. He drew a card, and held it up so that the captain could read what was on it.

"First steward," said the captain, reading it, and writing the position against the name in his book.

The next one was Tom Ridley, one of the Genverres boys. He drew "fourth fireman."

Dick Short was "starboard watch, No. 1."

"All the starboard watch have odd numbers, and the port even numbers," explained the captain.

Thad Glovering, of the Goldwing Club, drew "first officer." Corny Minkfield was first assistant-engineer. Pemberton Millweed was first cook. When Oscar Chester walked up to the pilot-house, there was a sensation among the boys that could not be wholly concealed. When he drew "second pilot" the sensation was more decided, though no one spoke; but all knew that he was to be associated intimately with Dory Dornwood.

CHAPTER XVII.

THE OFFICERS AND CREW OF THE SYLPH.

"WHO is first pilot, sir?" asked Oscar Chester while the captain was writing his name against his position.

"Dory Dornwood," replied Captain Gildrock.

Oscar made no reply; but, taking his card, he went to the main deck without a word of comment. It was not at all likely that the rebel would agree with the first pilot.

Captain Gildrock's book, when all had drawn their cards, and Dory had drawn one each for the two Plattsburgh pupils, gave the places as follows: —

First officer	THAD GLOVERING.
Second officer . . .	WILL ORWELL.
First pilot	DORY DORNWOOD.
Second pilot	OSCAR CHESTER.
Engineer	GEORGE JEPSON.
First assistant-engineer .	CORNY MINKFIELD.
Second assistant-engineer .	JOHN BRATTLE.
First fireman . . .	NAT LONG.

Second fireman	Dave Windsor.
Third fireman	Bolly Millweed.
Fourth fireman	Tom Ridley.
First cook	Pemberton Millweed.
Second cook	Jim Alburgh.
First steward	Bob Swanton.
Second steward	Steve Baxter.
Third steward	George Duane.
Fourth steward	Lick Milton.
Starboard watch	Dick Short.
Starboard watch	Phil Gawner.
Starboard watch	Ben Ludlow.
Port watch	Harry Franklin.
Port watch	Ned Bellows.
Port watch	Lew Shoreham.

"First and second officers, pilots, and engineers will return to the hurricane deck; the others will remain on the forecastle," said Captain Gildrock, when the cards had all been drawn.

The wheel had been given to Bates, and Dory had gone to the main deck with the others. The boys seemed to be in good humor, and those who had drawn inferior positions were apparently the jolliest of the crowd. Very likely they were disappointed: if they were, they did not complain.

The principal brought from the pilot-house a pile of coats and half a dozen badges, which he laid on a bench. As soon as the half-dozen he had called up had assembled near him, he spoke again.

"I told you there would be some changes in the uniform after we left Burlington," said he. "Those whom I have called up are to be regarded as officers. Instead of wearing the short jackets you have on, you will put on sack-coats. On his cap each of you will wear one of these badges, which indicates the position the wearer holds."

The officers put on the badges, and exchanged the short jackets for the more dignified garments handed to them by the captain. Certainly they looked more like officers than before. There was some good-natured chaffing among them, for they could not well help making fun of each other. As there was no appearance of ill-feeling among them, the principal did not object.

"What are we to do now, Captain Gildrock?" John Brattle asked.

"The first thing to do is to learn your duties," replied the captain. "You and Minkfield will go to the engine-room, and Mr. Jepson will instruct you."

The two engineers hastened below, full of enthusiasm, and very anxious to learn the duties of their new positions. The captain proceeded to instruct the first and second officers in regard to their offices, but all the time he was thinking about the second pilot. He was not prepared to send Oscar Chester into the pilot-house with Dory. But Bates knew how to steer; and knew the way to Plattsburgh; though he was not a pilot for the lake. Finally he concluded to send the second pilot to learn how to handle the wheel, while he kept Dory with him to assist in organizing the crew.

Captain Gildrock then went down to the main deck. The four firemen were immediately sent to the engineer. It happened that the two cooks had had some experience in their new department; and they were ordered to the galley, with instructions to learn all they could about the cooking arrangements, so that they could find any thing they wanted.

Pemberton Millweed had learned to cook a little, while with parties on the lake; and Jim Alburgh had spent one winter in a logging-camp in the woods, where he had learned the rudiments of the art. Both of them had a taste for this sort of thing; and, as soon as they had installed themselves in the galley, they were as happy as though they had drawn the cards bearing the titles of first and second officer.

The galley, or kitchen, was in the house on deck, with a glazed door on each side. The galley, or stove, from which the apartment takes its name, was forward of the doors. The after-end of the room was fitted up with a table, and a great number of lockers to contain every article needed in the art of cooking, except the meats and vegetables, which were in the ice-house, next to the galley. The two cooks, though strangers to each other until they met on board, were soon on excellent terms, and proceeded to make an examination of their new quarters.

Captain Gildrock next called out the three stewards, and conducted them to the forward cabin. The general duties of the stewards were to take care of the cabins, set the table, wait upon it at meals. One had not yet come on board.

"Then, we are to be sort of servants, are we?" said Lick Milton.

"We are all equal on board of the Sylph,"

replied the captain with a smile. "You are no more servants than all the others on the steamer. The first duty of officers and seamen is to obey orders; and the first officer is as much bound to do this as the stewards and deck-hands. It is as necessary to have our food good and well served as it is to navigate the vessel. You have as fair an opportunity to distinguish yourselves in this department as in any other. The officers may be waiters or stewards next month. In the course of time all the pupils will be required to discharge the duties of every department."

"How long do we have to serve as stewards?" asked Bob Swanton.

"I am not fully decided as to that: it will depend somewhat upon what progress you make. Probably we shall make some changes in a month. But this yacht is not the principal thing in the Beech-Hill Industrial School. We shall not go out in her every day in the week, perhaps not more than once a week after you have learned your duties."

"We are not to sail in her every day!" exclaimed Steve Baxter.

"Certainly not: after you have obtained a few

lessons in discipline on board of her, she will be a sort of plaything. But we shall make a trip every Saturday in her. On Monday morning we shall begin to put the shop in order, and go to work there as soon as we are ready."

"Then, we are not to have much fun," added Lick Milton.

"I hope you will all be pleased with your work in the shop and in the schoolroom," replied the captain. "On board of large vessels the chief steward is a person of no little consequence. He purchases the provisions and stores, and, in consultation with the first cook, makes out the bill of fare for each meal. All the other stewards obey his orders, and he is responsible for the condition of the cabin and the table. But I intended to put a sack-coat on you, Swanton, and give you a badge."

The chief steward went to the pilot-house with the captain, where he was provided with the sack and badge. He was directed to return to the cabin, and see that his department was in order, and all the stewards familiar with their work. Swanton was required to arrange with the cooks for a dinner for all on board, and to set the table for twelve persons. The principal gave them no minute instructions, preferring first to see what the chief steward would do without them.

Repairing to the forward deck with Dory, the captain found the six seamen, or deck-hands, waiting to be informed in regard to their duties. The first and second officers were called, for the work of the crew was to be supervised by them. They were to wash down the decks, and keep every thing outside of the cabins and engine and fire rooms in order. They were to learn to row the boats, heave the lead, to attend to the fasts in making a landing, to hoist and lower the boats, and to take their trick at the wheel.

They were divided into two watches, each being distinguished by a star on the right or left arm. Captain Gildrock was a practical man; and, as soon as he had explained the general duties of the crew, he required the decks to be washed down for the sake of the practice. By the aid of the steam-pump the planks were soon covered with water. They were scrubbed with brooms, and dried with swabs, the first and second officers superintending the work.

The boys worked as though they enjoyed it.

The sun soon dried the deck, and it looked as white as though it had been holystoned. The next lesson was in heaving the lead; and one by one the boys were mounted on the rail, and exercised till they could do it to the satisfaction of the principal.

It was now eleven o'clock, and the Sylph was half-way to Plattsburgh. It was necessary to see what had been done about dinner, and the captain went into the forward cabin. He found the three stewards on board very busy setting the table. They had found every thing they needed, and the table looked well. The principal encouraged the boys with some words of praise, and then went to the galley. There was a good fire in the range, and Pemberton Millweed was frying "chips."

The principal tasted the potatoes, and pronounced them excellent. The second cook was busy at the table preparing the vegetables. As both of them appeared to know what they were about, the captain asked no questions, and allowed the cooks and stewards to proceed with the dinner in their own way.

A visit to the engine-room revealed the fact that

Corny Minkfield, the first assistant-engineer, was in charge there, the chief-engineer being engaged in instructing the firemen in their duties. But Corny had been on steamers a great deal, and had some ideas in regard to machinery. He sat upon the sofa abaft the engine, and looked as dignified as though he had served in this department a dozen years.

In the fire-room Mr. Jepson was doing his duty faithfully. The firemen asked a great many questions, all of which were carefully answered. The second engineer was one of the party, for it was necessary that the engineers should fully understand the duties of the firemen. There was nothing for the principal to do, and he returned to the deck.

Dory was directed to take the wheel. When he went to the pilot-house, he found that Oscar Chester was steering the steamer. He was doing very well for a beginner, and the first pilot did not interfere.

CHAPTER XVIII.

ANOTHER BATTLE AT PLATTSBURGH.

DORY, without saying a word to Oscar, relieved Bates, and took his place at the starboard window in front. Captain Gildrock was pacing the hurricane deck, and the first pilot did not fear an attack from the rebel. But Oscar looked ugly, and bestowed savage glances upon his associate in the pilot-house.

"We shall get to Plattsburgh just at dinner-time," said Captain Gildrock, stopping at the door of the pilot-house.

"I suppose we can take dinner at the wharf as well as anywhere else," replied Dory.

"We shall not go up to the wharf; but we will keep the boat going till after dinner," added the captain. "What is your course, second pilot?"

"I am steering for that lighthouse ahead," replied Oscar.

"All right; but you may go to the eastward of it."

"What shall I steer for, sir?" inquired the second pilot.

"I don't know of any object near enough to guide you; but you can steer by compass, and make the course north by east," added the principal in a matter-of-fact way.

"I never steered by compass, sir, and I don't know how," said Oscar.

"That is one of the things a pilot ought to learn very early in his course. There is a compass in front of you on the shelf."

"I have seen it, but Bates told me to steer for that lighthouse."

"You did quite right. That is Cumberland Head light. You are steering just north by the compass, but there is a variation of the needle of about eleven and a half degrees. Now, port the helm until the point 'N. by E.' comes to the mark on the front of the case. Steer small," continued Captain Gildrock, placing himself by the side of the second pilot.

Oscar had learned enough of Bates to enable him to do this. He even knew that "steering small" was to move the wheel but a little at a time.

"That's right: now you have the steamer on her course. Remember, that, so far as any turning is concerned, the compass is stationary. It is the steamer, and not the compass, that turns, the needle always pointing to the north."

"I think I understand it, sir," replied Oscar.

But he did not, for the very first time he moved the wheel he turned it the wrong way.

"The other way, Chester," interposed the principal very gently. "You are doing first-rate, and you will soon get the hang of the new school-house."

Oscar reversed the movement of the wheel, and soon got the course again. He was wholly absorbed in his duty, and at that moment he had forgotten that Dory stood within a few feet of him. In a few minutes the second pilot got the nack of keeping the point for which he was steering on the mark.

"You are all right now, Chester," said the captain. "You will make a good pilot in due time."

"Thank you, sir," replied Oscar, who certainly appeared to have been greatly humanized by his experience on board.

The Sylph went along on her new course very

well. The second pilot had learned the art of steering small, and the steamer hardly wabbled at all. He kept his eyes fixed steadily on the compass, and the danger was that he would see nothing else. A small steamer was directly ahead, bound up the lake. Oscar did not appear to see her. Presently she blew one whistle. Dory waited for the second pilot to respond to the signal, but he did not appear to understand it. He had been shut up in the ice-house the night before when these signals were explained. Bates had had no occasion to instruct him in the manner of passing other steamers.

Dory pulled the line, and gave the required signal. Oscar looked at him with a scowl on his face, but neither of the pilots spoke. The little steamer sheered off, but hardly enough to pass the Sylph in safety. Dory did not like to interfere, lest he should give offence to the waspish associate in the pilot-house.

"Excuse me, Oscar Chester, but you must port the helm a little in order to pass that steamer," said Dory, when he found that his companion was likely to shave a hair off the approaching vessel.

"You are the first pilot, and I will obey whatever order you give me," replied Oscar in snappish tones, as he put the wheel to port.

"When a steamer blows one whistle, it is a signal that she intends to go to the starboard of us; and we have to reply with the one whistle," added Dory, glad to find that the second pilot could speak to him even in waspish tones.

"All right," growled Oscar.

At this moment one of the hands struck eight strokes, in couples, on the bell on the bitts. Bates had been explaining the bells to the crew.

"All the starboard watch will go to dinner now!" shouted Captain Gildrock.

The first officer and the second pilot were in the starboard watch. The engineer had arranged the watches to suit himself.

"I will relieve you while you are at dinner, Oscar Chester," said Dory, taking hold of the wheel.

"Thank you," replied Oscar gruffly, as he left the pilot-house.

Dinner was on the table in the forward cabin. The three stewards stood behind the chairs. The table looked as neat as that of a first-class hotel.

The linen was clean and white, the articles were arranged with good taste, and the dishes were neatly disposed in their proper places.

Captain Gildrock took his place at the head of the table, with the chief steward behind his chair. The first officer was directed to take the seat at the opposite end of the table. Mr. Jepson and Mr. Brookbine sat on the right and left of the captain, and the rest took such places as they chose.

The dinner was not an elaborate one, and both of the cooks were equal to such a meal every day in the week. In front of the captain was a dish of beefsteak, and before the first officer a platter of veal-cutlets. There were several kinds of vegetables, besides boiled potatoes and chips.

Every thing was well cooked; and the occupants of the galley declared that it ought to be, for both of them had done this thing times enough to learn how. The captain declared that Pemberton Millweed was good for something; and, if he would devote himself to the art of cooking, he could make more money in one year than he could in six as a counter-jumper. The captain said as much as this to him after dinner.

"But it is not quite so genteel," replied Pemberton with a smile.

"Genteel!" exclaimed the captain in a most contemptuous tone. "I will venture to say, that the cook of a first-class hotel in New York, not to mention many private families, is more genteel than any counter-jumper in Burlington. The most genteel man I ever saw was a journeyman barber. The bartenders cut the biggest swell in some cities. I can't see why a cook should not be as genteel as a counter-jumper, if he is so disposed. Male cooks get anywhere from six hundred to three thousand dollars a year, and they can better afford to be genteel than clerks on five to ten dollars a week."

The captain was rather curious to know what had happened at the house of Farmer Millweed after the poor man went home that morning, but he was not willing to ask either of the boys about it. The sons had both joined the school, and both were discharging their duties manfully. Doubtless there had been a stormy scene at the house of the farmer, and Mr. Millweed had risen somewhat in the estimation of the shipmaster.

The tables were set a second time at half-past twelve; and the port watch fared as well as the starboard, for, as far as practicable, a fresh meal had been cooked for its members. Mr. Jepson reported Bolingbroke as both willing and intelligent. He knew all about a steam-engine, and not a little about chemistry and the mathematics; for which the captain was willing to give the credit to the Genverres high-school.

Obeying the instructions of the captain, Dory had come about, and the steamer was headed up the lake. At Cumberland Head she changed her course again, and ran for Plattsburgh. At the north beacon on the breakwater, he rang to stop her. The second officer, prompted by the captain, had the anchor all ready to let go. The pilot gave the order when he was ready.

"Let go the anchor!" shouted Will Orwell.

Splash it went into the water: the Sylph swung around, and all hands were called. Captain Gildrock made a little speech to the boys, praised them for what they had done during the forenoon, and then gave them two hours' liberty to go on shore. He expected them to behave like gentlemen, and not disgrace the uniform they wore.

They were to be on the wharf at three o'clock, in readiness to return to the steamer.

The dummy exercise of lowering the boats was made real; and, with the exception of Jepson and Bates, all hands went on shore. No restraint was put upon them as to where they should go. Dory thought he would call upon some of his old friends in the place; and he started for the town, which is about three-quarters of a mile from the lake-shore. After he had passed the railroad-station, Oscar Chester suddenly presented himself before him. He had evidently been lying in wait for him.

"Dory Dornwood, we meet now on an equal footing; and I think I can keep my feet on the solid land as well as you can," said the second pilot savagely. "I promised to get even with you, and my time has come."

"If your time has come, Oscar Chester, my time has not gone," replied Dory calmly; and therein he had the advantage of the rebel. "I don't want to quarrel with you, and I won't if I can help it. I should like to talk the matter over with you, for I think you will be fair when you look on both sides of the question."

"I don't want to talk it over. You insulted

me last night, and then you caused me to be tumbled into the lake. I am going to have satisfaction; for I never forgive an insult," added Oscar, waxing fierce as his anger boiled within him.

"I did not intend to insult you; and I only did what any skipper would have done under the same circumstances," continued Dory.

"No more talk. I intend to thrash you here and now, till you say you have had enough of it, and are willing to beg my pardon," stormed Oscar, as he threw off his uniform sack, and tossed his badged cap upon the grass at the side of the road.

By this time a party of the ship's company came up. The second officer was in it; and, as soon as he understood what was going on, he hastened to the scene. He spoke to Oscar, and tried to induce him not to meddle with Dory. The others were not disposed to interfere with such a fellow as the second pilot. Will Orwell was his crony; and he persisted, taking his friend by the arm, and trying to lead him away.

"Don't talk to me, Will Orwell! You are half a traitor to me," said Oscar, shaking off his crony.

Without waiting for another word, the rebel leaped upon Dory. An instant later Oscar went over backwards, with the blood spurting from his nose. He sprang to his feet, and renewed the attack. In two minutes more he lay upon the ground, unable to rise.

CHAPTER XIX.

SOMETHING THAT HAPPENED ON SHORE.

OSCAR CHESTER was not killed, or even very seriously injured. The last blow of Dory had been planted in a sensitive place, and he had been stunned by it. His companions gathered around him, lifted him up, and procured some water from the Fouquet Hotel, with which they washed his head. In a few minutes his senses came back to him, and he was able to comprehend the situation.

Dory had been hit several times; but he was a tough youngster, and seemed to be none the worse for the battle. As he viewed the matter, he had simply defended himself, according to the first law of nature. He had done his best beforehand to avoid the fight, and had proposed to talk the matter over in order to ascertain who was to blame.

"That was an awful crack you gave him at the end," said Fireman Bolingbroke Millweed, joining

Dory, who stood alone on the grass. "I didn't know that you were such a hard hitter."

"I did not know it myself," replied Dory, wiping the perspiration from his brow. "I am not a fighting character, and I never struck a blow in my life except in self-defence."

"I think Chester has got enough of it," added the fireman.

"I don't know about that. He acts to me as though he was crazy. It would be just like him to pitch into me again as soon as he feels able to do so. I am sure I don't want to quarrel with him, especially as he is to be in the pilot-house with me. If I have done any thing out of the way, I am willing to beg his pardon; but he wouldn't even talk with me about his grudge against me."

"I saw the whole of it, and heard all that was said. I am sure you are not to blame," added Bolingbroke. "But I was glad to see you knock him out after he was so unreasonable."

"You were in the boat last night when the trouble began, and I hope you will be able to remember what passed between Oscar and me; for, after this, my uncle will be very likely to investigate the case."

"I remember all about it. Oscar wanted to steer the boat, and you objected. When he got up from his seat, — to take the helm, I suppose, — you told him to sit down; and you spoke rather sharply. Then the boat gave a lurch, and he went overboard. If it hadn't been for you, Dory, he would have been drowned as sure as fate," replied Bolingbroke, rehearsing the facts precisely as they were.

"I am ready to face the music, and if I have done any thing wrong I shall be glad to apologize for it. In this fight, I only defended myself, as I think every fellow ought to do."

"How are you, Dory?"

The pilot looked around, and saw Mr. Peppers, a constable of Plattsburgh, who sometimes did detective work. He had sailed down the lake with Dory in the Goldwing a few weeks before, and Peppers had a strong regard for the skipper.

"I am glad to see you, Mr. Peppers," replied Dory, shaking hands with the detective.

"You have settled that fellow so that he won't want any more of your love-pats," replied Peppers, laughing. "I saw the whole of it, and it was handsomely done."

"I merely defended myself. He pitched into

me, and I could not help myself," answered the pilot in the language and tone of apology; for he did not want any one to think that he ever engaged in a voluntary fight.

"I know it: I saw the whole of it. You were trying to talk with him when he rushed upon you," added Peppers.

By this time Oscar Chester appeared to have recovered from the heavy blows of his brother pilot. He and Will Orwell walked up the street towards the town. The excitement was all over, and the other pupils scattered. Peppers followed Chester. Dory was doubtful what to do. At first he thought of going on board of the Sylph, and reporting the battle to his uncle.

After a little consideration, and some talk with Bolingbroke about it, he decided not to do so. He was ready to answer to any charge that might be brought against him, and it would be time enough to defend himself when he was accused. He called at the Witherill House, had a chat with the landlord and the clerk, and then returned to the wharf. By this time most of the boys had seen all they wanted to of the town, and were ready to go on board. Captain Gildrock had come on shore, and had just gone on board with the two Plattsburgh boys who were to join the school.

Bates was in charge of the boats; and, as soon as the crew of one of them appeared, he sent one load on board. The principal was instructing the two new hands, who had already put on the uniform. One was a steward, and the other belonged to the port watch.

At a little after three o'clock the other boat came off, and the students rushed up the accommodation steps as though they enjoyed the steamer and the lake more than the town. George Duane, the new steward, was handed over to Bob Swanton, after a proper introduction; and they retired to the forward cabin.

"Have all hands come on board?" asked Captain Gildrock.

The boys looked about them, as though they were unable to answer the question.

"You don't know: well, we can soon ascertain by calling the roll," added the principal, as he took the list of students from his pocket. "Mr. Glovering."

"Here sir," replied the first officer in the midst

of the laughter of the boys when they heard the handle applied to his name.

"Mr. Orwell."

"Here, sir."

"Mr. Dornwood."

"Here, sir."

"Mr. Chester."

There was no response to this name, and it was repeated. There was no answer.

"Is the second pilot on board?" asked Captain Gildrock; and Dory wondered if he knew anything about the second battle of Plattsburgh.

The first and second officers looked about the deck and into the cabins for the missing pilot, but he could not be found. A more thorough search was made by all hands, and it was soon evident that "Mr. Chester" was not on board. The captain finished the call of the roll, and made no remark in regard to the disappearance of the second pilot. He directed the first officer to get up the anchor.

It looked as though Oscar Chester had absconded, notwithstanding his good conduct during the forenoon. Possibly some of the boys, especially Will Orwell, knew something about the matter; but they did not volunteer to give any information, and the principal did not ask for any. He said nothing at all, in fact, about the missing student. The captain did not appear to be in the least degree disturbed by the absence of the refractory pupil.

Captain Gildrock looked on while the crew walked around the capstan. The officers had learned their lesson well; and, for a first trial, the operation of getting up the anchor was handsomely done.

The first pilot was at his post; and, as soon as "anchor aweigh" was reported to him, he rang the gong. Mr. Jepson stood on deck, near the door of the engine-room, having stationed his first assistant at the machine. He opened the valve slowly, and the thumping of the screw was immediately heard.

Captain Gildrock had gone to the hurricane deck, where he could see all that was done in the pilot-house and on the forecastle. He cast occasional glances at the wharf, and he directed Dory to run in that direction. Then he called the first officer, and told him to get ready to make a landing.

Dory ran the Sylph up to the wharf, where she was secured by the enthusiastic crew. The portion of the bulwark at the starboard gangway was removed, and the plank run out. While Mr. Glovering was wondering who was going on shore, Oscar Chester stepped out of the building on the wharf, and walked on board as coolly as though nothing had happened to disturb his equanimity.

"Haul in the plank!" called the captain. "Cast off, Dory."

The pilot on duty blew a sharp whistle, which was the signal to cast off the fasts; and the officers below attended to this duty. The Sylph backed out from the wharf, and then went ahead, the engine being wholly managed by Corny Minkfield. Oscar Chester went directly to the hurricane deck, and was about to enter the pilot-house, when he was confronted by Captain Gildrock.

"You are late, Mr. Chester," said the principal.

"I came on board against my will, sir. In fact, I was brought down to the wharf," replied Oscar.

"Indeed? Who brought you to the wharf?" asked the captain with a half-suppressed chuckle.

"I wasn't introduced to him, but he said he was a constable."

"You ought to have been introduced to him," laughed the captain. "I can't go through the ceremony now, because the constable is not here; but his name is Peppers. Dory knows him, and he will introduce you if I don't happen to be present when you meet again. Am I to understand from what you say that you did not intend to return to the steamer?"

"I did not intend to return: on the contrary, I meant to run away; for I suppose that is what you would call it," replied Oscar.

"If I remember rightly, you promised this morning to behave as well as you knew how, if I released you from the brig," added the captain.

"I meant what I said at the time, and intended to keep my promise; but something happened on shore that prevented me from doing so," replied Oscar rather sheepishly for him.

"What is the matter with your face, Mr. Chester? Your nose is swelled, and you have a mouse under each eye. I should say that both of your eyes would be in mourning for the next week," added Captain Gildrock.

"The black eyes are in consequence of something that happened on shore," answered the second pilot.

"What was that?"

"Excuse me, sir: if you will ask Dory, he can tell the story better than I can," replied Oscar, glancing at the pilot at the wheel.

This conversation took place at the door of the pilot-house, and Dory could not help hearing all that was said; and if he looked behind him he could see the parties.

"I prefer that you should tell your own story," added the principal rather sternly. "My business just now is with you and not with Dory."

"To make a short story of it, sir, I attempted to thrash Dory, and I got thrashed myself," answered the culprit.

"Served you right!" exclaimed the captain. "Have you settled the matter finally?"

"It seems to have settled itself, sir. I had no doubt I could whip Dory as easily as I could turn my hand. I never met one of these proper fellows before that I could not whip, and without the least difficulty. I am satisfied now that he can whip me every time, and that settles the matter."

"I should say that you judge yourself and Dory by a very mean and cowardly standard. But if you are satisfied, nobody else need complain this time. Return to your duty, Mr. Chester."

Oscar went to the wheel, and did not seem to have any delicacy about meeting Dory.

CHAPTER XX.

THE NEW HEAD OF THE MILLWEED FAMILY.

CAPTAIN GILDROCK judged, from the appearance of Oscar Chester's face, that he had been severely punished for his assault upon his superior officer. He had not heard a word about the second battle at Plattsburg. Though Bates knew all about it, he never meddled with what did not concern him.

He walked away from the pilot-house, satisfied that Dory could take care of himself if the second pilot wanted any thing more of him. Mr. Jepson had divided the firemen into watches, and two of them were now off duty. The principal saw Bolingbroke walking the hurricane deck, and called him. In answer to his question, Bolingbroke told him all the particulars of the fight on shore. Of course the statement was highly favorable to Dory.

If no one else knew it, the principal did, that Will Orwell was a crony of the second pilot. From him he could get the other side of the story, if there was any other side to it; and he called the second officer. Orwell's story did not differ materially from that of the fireman, and the captain was satisfied that the assault upon his nephew had been entirely unprovoked. He knew all about the difficulty in the boat, and on board of the steamer the night before.

The captain was satisfied that Chester had been sufficiently punished, especially when he considered what a shock the pride of the wilful boy had received in his failure to thrash Dory. Doubtless his attempt to run away had been caused by his defeat. He was humiliated and mortified at the result.

Of course Peppers did not act without instructions. The principal expected a demonstration on the part of the rebel. He had written to the officer the day before, requesting him to be on the wharf when the Sylph arrived, and instructing him to watch Oscar all the time the latter was on shore. He was to bring him off if he attempted to run away.

Peppers soon ascertained which of the boys he was to "shadow," and followed him wherever he went. Orwell remained in his company till it was time to return to the wharf. Oscar declared that he would not go on board again, and tried to induce his crony to join him in his flight into the country.

Orwell was second officer, and was delighted with his experience in the Beech-Hill Industrial School so far. It was better than a play to him, and nothing could have induced him to run away from the agreeable life which had just opened upon him. He had reasoned with his friend very earnestly, and even had the pluck to tell him flatly that Dory was altogether in the right, and he was altogether in the wrong.

Oscar admitted that he was pleased with the school, but he could not endure the humiliation of playing "second fiddle" to Dory after what had happened. They parted, and Orwell went on board with the other pupils; and he was utterly astonished when he saw his crony come on board at the wharf.

"If you wish to steer, I will give you the wheel, Oscar Chester," said Dory, when the second pilot had been in the room a few minutes. "It is not a new thing to me; and I am not anxious to steer, though I like to do it well enough."

"Thank you, Dory Dornwood: you are very kind. You can whip me every time; and, of course, you can bully me if you have a mind to do so," replied Oscar, beginning very stiffly.

"I have no wish to bully you or any other fellow. I don't want to quarrel with any person; and, as we are to be in the pilot-house together, I hope we shall be able to agree," added Dory in the most conciliatory tones.

"We shall agree after this," said Oscar, letting himself down a few pegs. "You can whip me, and that is enough. I can't quarrel with you without getting the worst of it. I must submit, and I may as well make the best of it."

"I don't believe in fighting, and I don't care a straw who is the best man. I don't mean to bully even the weakest fellow in the school. I know I speak quick sometimes, but I don't mean any thing by it. I am told that I spoke rather sharply to you in the boat last night. I am sorry for it, and I beg your pardon," said Dory.

"You don't owe me any apology after you have whipped me; and you are generous to let me down as easily as you can," added Oscar.

"It was since we came on board, after the affair,

that I was told I spoke sharply to you. If you had told me so before hitting me, I should have begged your pardon. I mean to do the right thing."

"Your hand, Dory!" exclaimed Oscar, extending his own. "You are a good fellow, even if you are so frightfully proper."

Dory gave the rebel his right hand, and his companion shook it heartily. There was some good left in Oscar Chester.

"I always thrashed every fellow in the school that didn't fag to me, and I suppose I have been spoiled. But I will try to do better. If I don't do well, you must thrash me again, Dory," added the second pilot, smiling blandly. "I hope we shall be friends; and I will take the wheel now, if you will show me how to handle it."

"You handle it very well already, though there are a great many things you will have to learn, as every wheelman must," replied Dory cordially, and without putting on any airs.

There was peace in the pilot-house now, as there was in every part of the steamer. Captain Gildrock looked into the room after a while, and found that the two pilots were apparently excellent friends. He did not say any thing, or even enter the apartment; for he thought the boys would get along better without any help.

The Sylph went up the lake as far as Ticonderoga. The instruction was continued in all the departments; and as the students were required to do the work themselves, as well as listen to the theory, they made rapid progress, and enjoyed themselves to the end of the trip. They were sorry when it was finished.

The steamer was secured at the temporary wharf in Beech Lake. Supper had been served on board, as arranged in the morning; and the cooks and stewards had to put things in order before they went on shore. The engineers and firemen were taught in what shape to leave the engine and boilers. The first and second officers put the decks in order. But the pilots had nothing to do when the boat touched the wharf.

"Is Captain Gildrock on board?" asked Mr. Millweed, who was on the wharf when Dory landed.

"He is in the after cabin," replied the first pilot; and he would have been very glad to hear what passed between the principal and the farmer.

But he had been taught to mind his own business; and he walked up to the dormitory with Oscar, who had not yet visited the room appropriated to his use. Mr. Millweed went on board of the Sylph, and found the captain at the desk in his room.

"I will wait till you are ready to see me, Captain Gildrock," said he.

"I am ready to see you now, and anxious to hear what you have to say," replied the principal, as he led the way out of the state-room into the main cabin. "Both of the boys came on board before nine, and have done well. Pemberton is first cook, and Bolingbroke is third fireman."

"I suppose they don't like these places," added Farmer Millweed.

"Both of them seem to be very well satisfied. Pemberton is an excellent cook," answered the captain. "He thinks his position is not particularly genteel, but he will get over that in a short time. Did Mrs. Millweed consent to their joining the school?"

"She did not: she objected with all her might. But I saw that the boys were inclined to go to the school. We had a regular row, but I stuck to my text; and finally I told the boys I could not support them another day in idleness.

"My wife cried; but I told her it was no use, for we should all be turned out of the house, and all that I had would be sold to pay my debts. I told the boys to hurry down here before the boat started; and they minded me, in spite of the screams of my wife. It made me feel bad, but I couldn't help it."

"I am sorry you had any trouble, but I think you have done right," added Captain Gildrock.

"When the boys had gone, I had a talk with the girls. I told them the plain truth, and insisted that they should go to work. Both of them said they were willing; but their mother declared they should not go into a store or factory, or any thing of that sort, to work. They had been finely educated, and were fit to adorn the drawing-room of a rich man."

"Very likely they are; but the next thing is to find the drawing-room," suggested the captain.

"That is the very thing I said to Matilda — that's my wife. I told the girls I would try to find places, and they both said they would take any places I could get for them. Matilda said they should not. I told them I had not money enough to buy a meal of victuals, and the storekeepers and the butchers won't trust me. I found a place in a store for Elinora myself; and she went to it, after dinner, to-day."

"Excellent! You are doing bravely!" exclaimed the captain. "I will see what can be done for the other girl as soon as I go ashore. By the way, I was thinking of getting a young man to keep the records of the school, and do some of my writing for me. A woman will do just as well. I will give your other daughter five dollars a week, and raise her wages as fast as she learns to do the work."

"God bless you, Captain Gildrock!" ejaculated the discouraged father. "If the children can support themselves, I can take care of my wife after we have lost the farm and every thing else. I can get work at day wages."

"I hope you won't lose your farm," added the captain.

"There is no help for it. The mortgage note will be due in a short time; and I can't pay the interest, let alone any part of the principal."

Farmer Millweed groaned in spirit, when he thought of the final blow that was about to fall upon him. He had been an honest, temperate, hard-working man all his life, though he was a person of but little force of character. His wife's aspirations after gentility had actually ruined him. As things were going on the day before, the family were only a few steps from the poor-house.

"I think you are an honest man, and I am very sorry to see you brought to the verge of ruin in this way," said Captain Gildrock after a few minutes' reflection. "I will let you have the money to pay your interest when it is due, and I will take the mortgage on your place myself."

"I did not expect any thing of this sort from you, captain; and I am sure "—

"Never mind that, Mr. Millweed. If any of your creditors trouble you, come to me. You have got rid of the principal trouble; and there is no reason why you should not do well, — pay all your debts, and clear off the mortgage on your farm."

The farmer was profuse in his expressions of gratitude; but the captain cut them short by inquiring still further into his affairs, and giving him much good advice. Mr. Millweed went home with hope in his soul. There was a new head to the Millweed family.

CHAPTER XXI.

CAPTAIN GILDROCK ARGUES AGAINST HIGH-SCHOOLS.

THE next day was Sunday; and Captain Gildrock insisted that all the students should attend church, and refrain from all work and play. Those who lived in Genverres were allowed to spend the day at home. No excursions on the river or the lake were permitted, and no scholar was allowed even to get into any of the boats.

On Monday morning the actual work of the school was begun. The study-hours were from nine till twelve in the forenoon. The two gentlemen who were to teach in the scholastic department had arrived, and promptly at the hour the school was called to order.

"Now, my lads, we are ready for work," said the captain on the platform. "I am told that you can all read, write, and cipher. You have some knowledge of geography and history. I dare say, some of you have studied Greek, Latin,

French, and German, which are all very well in their place; but we shall have nothing to do with them here. We are to make good mechanics of you, and not good scholars."

"Can't good scholars be good mechanics?" asked Bolingbroke Millweed.

"Certainly they can: I don't object to any amount of scholarship," replied Captain Gildrock rather warmly. "You have been to the high-school, Bolingbroke; but all that you have learned will not prevent you from becoming a first-class mechanic. On the contrary, your education will be a great help to you."

"That is just what I thought," added the graduate of the high-school.

"For two or three years an exciting question has been under discussion here in Genverres," continued the principal, turning to the two instructors. "I have taken the practical side of the subject, and I don't believe in sending all the boys and girls to the high-school. When our fathers here in New England planted the school-house by the side of the church, I don't believe they meant a high-school."

"Of course not: such an institution was unknown in their day, — at least, as we understand it," replied Mr. Bentnick. "They simply meant an ordinary common-school education, as we call it now."

"That must be all they meant; but there has been progress in education, as in every thing else, since their time," added Mr. Darlingby.

"I rejoice in the progress as much as any one can," retorted the captain vigorously. "But I believe there is intemperance in the matter of education as well as in eating and drinking. The first business of life, in an enlightened or a savage state, is bread and butter. In other words, a man must get his living before he does any thing beyond that; and the greater part of our population can do nothing more than get a living. Do you believe that, boys?"

The boys did believe it, though none of them had ever given much attention to social and political economy. It was plain enough that the first duty of existence for every person was to support himself.

"But some are born rich," suggested Corny Minkfield.

"Then their means of support are provided,

but this is not the case with one in a hundred. The great body of our people have to earn their own living. The only real objections I have to the high-school are, first, that it unfits boys and girls for the humble labors of life; and, second, that it uses up so many of the years of the young in learning what does not directly help them in earning their own livelihood," continued the captain.

"But what they learn in the high-school is a direct help to them in all the business of life," suggested Mr. Darlingby.

"Boys and girls spend their time from fourteen or sixteen years of age, till they are eighteen or twenty, in learning Latin, French, German, literature, the higher mathematics, and such branches, when they might learn a trade, or obtain a knowledge of business. When they graduate, they don't want to learn a trade, work on a farm, or do manual labor of any kind. They look down upon such occupations. They want to be clerks, if they are boys, or marry wealthy men, if they are girls. They must do something, if any thing at all, that is genteel."

"There is a great deal of truth in that statement," added Mr. Bentnick. "Boys don't stay in the country, and work on the farm, now as they did fifty years ago."

"I had a curiosity, when I was in New York last spring, to inquire into the salaries paid to clerks and salesmen in dry-goods stores," continued the captain. "So far as I could obtain the information, the average was not above ten dollars a week. Of course, some got two or three thousand dollars a year, or even double these sums; but I found that a great many young men worked for five or six dollars a week, and some for even less. Good mechanics earned from ten to thirty dollars a week.

"Why, a common laborer got from six to twelve dollars a week. While mechanics and laborers were in demand, there were multitudes of counter-jumpers, and other persons who wanted what they called genteel occupations, who could get nothing to do. In a word, our institutions of learning have fitted too many for the so-called higher grades of employment."

"But sometimes the mechanics and laborers are out of work?" said Bolingbroke.

"They are, for it sometimes happens that over-production shuts up the shops and manufactories.

But these men have been taught to work with their hands, and their bodies have been fitted for such service. When they can't get work at their trades, they do something else. Thousands upon thousands of them go to the great West, and become farmers. They can always get a living out of the earth, if they can't any other way. But I did not intend to argue this question; though I desire every young man to think for himself, and form his own opinions. You can think as you please; and if you believe that high-schools, as managed at the present time, promote the best interests of the whole people, you are entirely welcome to your opinion."

"My father don't believe in high-schools, and would not send me to one," said Phil Gawner.

"Never mind what your father believes: make up your mind yourself, and have your own opinions, my lad. Now, boys, the studies you are to pursue here are those which will fit you to become good mechanics. But I hope you will read and study as long as you live. What I intend to do is to fit you out with a business that will enable you to earn your own living."

Miss Fatima Millweed was present with the

record-books with which she had been provided; and the name, age, and residence of each pupil were taken. The average age of the scholars was found to be fourteen and a half. A few were only twelve, but several were eighteen and nineteen. All of them were graduates of grammar-schools, and some had attended high-schools and academies. Of course, the schools they had attended did not fairly gauge their attainments; for some of the oldest, who had been to the higher schools of learning, were weak in knowledge and mental power when compared with the ones who had only been to the lower grades of schools.

"Now, my lads, a few words more, and I shall leave you to your instructors. The studies you will pursue are all practical ones," said the captain, taking the platform again. "The principal branches will be drawing, natural philosophy, chemistry, geometry, and book-keeping. Geography, history, arithmetic, and grammar will be taught incidentally. Before you graduate, there will be a course in botany, geology, and zoölogy. At one o'clock you will all assemble in the shop, and make a beginning in the mechanical part of your education."

The captain left the platform, and left the schoolroom. Mr. Bentnick was the chief instructor, Mr. Darlingby being his assistant. He proceeded to organize the classes in the studies the principal had mentioned. He made such rules as he considered necessary, but they were not very stringent.

The boys were divided into two classes, according to their attainments. Ten were found who had made considerable progress in the four principal studies, and these were the first class. Mr. Bentnick proceeded to give them a lecture in chemistry. It was conversational, and the instructor soon found where to make a beginning in the science.

At the same time Mr. Darlingby began with the rudiments in the second class. The pupils were provided with text-books, and lessons assigned for the next day. A start was made in geometry in the same manner, and by that time it was noon. At quarter past twelve the dinner-bell rang; and all hands, including the family, the instructors, the pupils, and Miss Millweed, seated themselves at the long table. It was a sociable meal; and no one seemed to be under any restraint, though the boys behaved very well.

Mr. Darlingby had something more to say in favor of high-schools, in which he had been a teacher for several years. He wanted to know if Captain Gildrock believed that the higher branches should be taught at the public expense.

"I think the expense is the least important part of the subject," replied the principal; "but I will answer the question. I do not believe that high-schools should be supported, as a rule, out of the public taxes."

"You are very radical in your opinions, Captain Gildrock," added the instructor.

"Let us look at it a moment. There are two thousand scholars of all ages in the public schools of Genverres. Not more than one in five of them will ever reach the highest class in the grammar-school. The other four will leave school, and go to work: their parents need them, or what they can earn. But the parents of all those who fall out of the schools by the way are tax-payers. Some are only poll-taxes, but a few of them pay on their little lots of land and houses. It costs about five times as much to educate a pupil in the high-school as in the elementary schools. The parents of four-fifths of the scholars can't afford even to send their children through the grammar-school course, to say nothing of the high-school; but they have to pay their share of the expenses of the high-school, which I contend is not just."

"But the safety of our institutions depends upon the education of the people," replied Mr. Darlingby.

"Does it depend upon a college education? Why not insist that every person should be a graduate of a college, and that no person could be moral and upright without having a college degree?" added the principal.

"There is reason in all things."

"You draw the line after the high-school, and I before: that is the only difference. It would be as just to support the colleges at the public expense as the high-schools. The education that preserves the State is not French and German, Latin and Greek, chemistry and physics; but it is the education that distinguishes the immigrant who cannot read and write from the farmers and mechanics of this country. It does not include a high-school training."

"Then, if a poor man's son or daughter, with a taste for learning, wants an education, he shall not have it because his father cannot pay for it," added Mr. Darlingby warmly and indignantly.

"You have struck the weak point of my argument, sir," replied the principal. "I would have scholarships provided by the State for such pupils."

Dinner was over, and the company left the table.

CHAPTER XXII.

THE CHAMPLAIN MECHANICS IN THE SHOP.

THE boys had listened with interest to the discussion at the dinner-table; and, when they gathered in front of the shop, they were talking about the subject themselves. But they were hardly ready to settle their opinions in the matter. The principal's views sounded very much like heresy to some of them, who had been taught that it was the most praiseworthy thing in the world to attend the high-school. They were in doubt; and, in this respect, they were like thousands of full-grown women and men.

When Mr. Jepson unlocked the doors of the shop, there was a general rush for the inside of it. High-school education was forgotten, and everybody's curiosity was excited to know what the mechanical school was to be.

The master-carpenter and the engineer, assisted by Bates and other men who worked on the estate, had placed all the boxes of carpenter's tools in the shop; but not one of them had yet been opened. The benches were all that looked like furniture. Of these there were half a dozen for wood-work, and a dozen for iron. Overhead were the shafts, drums, and pulleys by which various machines were to be operated.

"Here we are again, my lads," said Captain Gildrock, standing upon one of the boxes. "The first thing to be done is to put the shop in order. Your instructors are here; and you must heed what they say, and obey their orders. Like the session of the forenoon, the afternoon will last three hours. At four o'clock you will be dismissed for the rest of the day. The time will be your own then, but you must learn the lessons which have been assigned. Now, Mr. Brookbine and Mr. Jepson, I turn the pupils over to you. They have already been divided into classes. Mr. Jepson will take the first, and Mr. Brookbine the second."

Captain Gildrock stepped down from the box, and seated himself on one of the benches to witness the proceedings. He was quite as much interested as any of the pupils.

"I am to teach you the use of carpenter's tools,"

said Mr. Brookbine. "It will be an easy and pleasant job if you give attention and try to do the best you can. The tools we have here are of the latest fashion, and some of them are quite different from those with which I learned my trade.

"Let me say, that every one of them must be handled with the utmost care, and be kept in good order. You will be shown how to grind upon the grindstone, and sharpen on the oil-stone, the chisels and plane-irons. None but a bad workman ever uses dull tools. It is easier to avoid running your tools against a nail than it is to grind out the gaps the nail will make."

"But where are the tools? I don't see any," asked Tom Ridley.

"They are in these boxes, and we will now open them. I will put two of you to each box, for there are just six of these large boxes. Dory and Thad Glovering may begin with the first one: the others will look on, and see how it is done. You may learn how to do it, or how not to do it."

The carpenter handed Dory and Thad a wooden mallet, a chisel, and a hatchet. Thad was full of enthusiasm. He thought he knew just how to do it. He had the hatchet and chisel in his hands. Inserting the latter under the lid of the box at one end, he struck the handle of the chisel with the hatchet.

"Stop there, if you please," interposed Mr. Brookbine.

Thad looked at the carpenter with astonishment, for he had no suspicion that there was any thing wrong in what he had done.

"What I say to Thad I say to the whole class," continued the carpenter. "He has done just what most of you would if you had been in his place. What is that mallet for, Thad?"

"To hit with, just as your fist is," replied the amateur workman, laughing.

"To strike with, and that is just what your fist is not for. You are never to strike a wooden tool, or the wooden handle of a tool, with a hammer or a hatchet. Can you all remember that, my lads?"

"Yes, sir!" shouted all the boys.

"Don't do it, then. A mallet is used in striking a chisel."

Thad took the mallet, and hit the chisel a tremendous crack with it. The tool happened to be in a rather loose place in the opening, and it went in to the handle. Thad tried to draw it out. He pulled and tugged and wrenched at the chisel, but it was in firm enough to resist all his efforts. He was so much in earnest, that his attempts amused the rest of the boys; and they were soon laughing with all their might. The machinists at the other end of the shop were interested, and some of them went over to see what the excitement was. But they were called back by Mr. Jepson before they could see inside of the ring that surrounded Thad.

"Pull away, my lad," laughed the master-carpenter. "But when you get tired of the work, let me know, if you please."

"I can't get it out," replied Thad, when he discovered that he was the laughing-stock of the class.

"Perhaps you can, if you keep on wrenching for a day or two longer."

"I have done my best, and it won't come out."

"I don't think it will under any such treatment," added Mr. Brookbine. "You laugh, boys, because it is funny; but I doubt if the majority of you would have done any better. Here is a lesson to learn. Skill is better than strength, but skill and strength win the battle."

"Good!" shouted Steve Baxter. "I will remember that as long as I live: skill and strength win the battle."

"I hope you will all remember it, for it is just the motto for a carpenter. The 'improvement,' as the minister would say, upon the text, is this: When things don't work right, and won't do as you want and expect them to do, don't yank, twist, jerk, and wrench at them. Something is the matter, and you must see what it is. That chisel would not come out. Why not?"

"It is in too tight," replied Dick Short.

"Right, Dick: what is to be done?"

"Loosen it, if you can."

"Dory, you may try your hand at it, taking the chisel as you find it."

Dory had been studying the situation, and had made up his mind what to do. Taking the hatchet, he inserted the edge of it in the crack, near the chisel, and drove it in with the mallet. The chisel dropped out of itself. But the hatchet stuck as hard as the chisel had.

"Good, so far, Dory; but your chisel is in chancery," said the carpenter.

"What is sauce for goose is sauce for gander,"

replied Dory as he picked up the chisel, and inserted it in the opening made by the hatchet. Twisting the hatchet a little, he started the nails with which the cover of the box was secured.

In the manner described, Dory alternately used the tools till he had gone half-way round the box, when he and Thad took hold of the board with their hands, and pulled it off.

"That was very well done," said the carpenter. "But the board could have been taken off without pulling it off with the hands."

"I know it, Mr. Brookbine; but that was the quicker way to do it," replied Dory.

"So it was. It is quicker to pick up a rock, if you can, than to hoist it with a machine," added Mr. Brookbine. "Now, Corny Minkfield, you and Nat Long may open the next one."

These operators had closely observed the method of Dory, and they opened the box without any difficulty. The others were disposed of in the same manner. The boys turned to the instructor for the next step in the interesting proceedings.

"These boxes contain six sets of carpenter's tools," said Mr. Brookbine. "I shall describe them to you as they are taken from the cases.

The tools are all packed in the same order. Dory will pass me the first package, and those who have opened the boxes will take the same bundle from each of them."

Dory took a thin package from the top of the box. Removing the paper from it, he handed the tool to the carpenter.

"I needn't tell you what this is, for you all know," continued Mr. Brookbine.

"It looks very much like a saw," said Thad. "I know what it is, and what it is for."

"I am glad you do, Thad, though I have my doubts. Will you look at it, and tell me what kind of a saw it is?"

Thad took the implement; and, putting on a very wise expression, he examined it carefully.

"I should say that this was a hand-saw," said he at last.

"Quite right: it is a hand-saw. Why is that name given to it — to distinguish it from what?"

"From the saw in a saw-mill, or a circular-saw, which is not a hand-saw," answered Thad.

"You have answered as well as could be expected. There is no particular meaning to the name, and the term is seldom used. There are not a few words that lose their original meaning. I suppose if I should ask you to go for a wood-saw, you would know what I meant."

"I should say you meant the one used to saw fire-wood," replied Thad.

"Precisely so; but all the saws in these boxes are wood-saws. Mr. Jepson has saws for sawing brass and iron; but the term 'wood-saw,' or 'buck-saw,' was not given to distinguish it from them. If I asked you to saw off the end of the board you have taken off the box, do you think you could do it with this saw, Thad?"

"I think I could: in fact, I have no doubt of it," replied Thad confidently.

"Suppose you try it; but don't saw through any of the nails."

Dory assisted him to place the board in a proper position on the box. The amateur commenced operations, but the saw did not work as well as he expected. In spite of all his efforts, it would jump out of its place; and it would not cut at all well.

"I don't think this saw has ever been filed," said Thad, disgusted with the ill success of his efforts.

"The saw is sharp, well set, and in good order," replied Mr. Brookbine. "Can any one of you tell me what kind of a saw this is?"

"It is a slitting-saw," answered Dory and two or three others, who had been examining the saws taken from the other boxes.

"That's what's the matter," laughed the carpenter. "It was not made to cut across the grain, and it will not do it very well. With this saw you work *with* the grain of the wood, and it is never used for any other purpose. You will all have a chance to try it in a day or two. — The next package, Dory. — Another saw," added the instructor, as he took the tool in his hand. "Can any of you tell me what kind of a saw this is?"

"It is a cutting-off saw," said Nat Long.

"Right. It is also called a panel-saw, when it has fine teeth. If you compare the filing and setting of the two saws, you will see that the teeth of the last are of a different angle from the other, and that it has more set than the slitting-saw; that is, the teeth are thrown out more. — What next, Dory?"

Just then there was a roar of laughter from the machine-shop.

CHAPTER XXIII.

SOMETHING ABOUT TOOLS AND WORK.

IF there was any thing funny, the boys all wanted to know what it was; and some of them were inclined to run over to ascertain why the young machinists were laughing. Mr. Brookbine suspended his instructions, and seated himself on one of the benches.

"Shall we appoint a committee to ascertain what is going on at the other end of the shop, or shall we all go over and see for ourselves?" said the carpenter.

"We must have a partition between the two shops," added Captain Gildrock. "Just now half the machinists started to come over here."

"The partition would be a nuisance; and, after a while, the boys will probably get tired of laughing at each other's blunders," added the carpenter: and by this time the class were all giving attention. "What next, Dory?"

Dory unfolded another package, which was

found to contain another saw. Mr. Brookbine took it, and held it up before the pupils.

"You all know that this is a saw, but what is the name of it?" he asked.

"I have always heard it called a fine saw," answered Jim Alburgh.

"It is often called so, but I have shown you that names don't always describe the object to which they are applied. Some saws made like the cutting-off saw have finer teeth than this one, — the panel-saw, for instance. There is another and better name, which applies to all saws of this kind; and, if you please, we will call it the back-saw. You see that it has a steel back to prevent it from bending, as all without it will do. — The next article."

This proved to be another back-saw, but not more than half as long or wide as the first one. It was for finer work, and could very properly be called a fine saw. The carpenter required the next four packages to be opened before he said any thing about their contents.

"These are planes," said he, when he had placed them on a bench where all the class could see them. "These four are the ones in common use, but you cannot fully understand them until you have used them a while. We will examine the one that is used first, and here it is;" and Mr. Brookbine took up one of the tools. "What should you call this?"

"A fore-plane," replied Dick Short.

"That is as good a name for it as any other, but this is a jack-plane. It is used to take off the rough side or edge of the board. It is fifteen inches long. What the manufacturers call a fore-plane is eighteen or twenty inches long. In this country very few carpenters use both: and, whichever one it may be, some call it a jack-plane, and some a fore-plane; the latter being the most common name in this part of the country.

"When I learned my trade, boards were brought into the shop just as they came from the saw-mill. Now they are generally planed by machinery, so that the hardest part of your work will be done before you get the board. Here is a short plane, only eight and a half inches long. What do you call it?"

"A smoothing-plane. It is used to polish off the board after you have taken off the rough," replied Corny Minkfield.

"Hardly to polish it, though I understand what you mean. We don't polish wood with a plane: we simply smooth it."

"That is what I meant," added Corny.

"If polishing various kinds of wood were not a part of the cabinet-maker's business, I should have said nothing; but we must learn to use words that correctly convey our meaning, when we can just as well as not. The smoothing-plane is used after the rough has been taken off the board. This is the next plane in the series," continued Mr. Brookbine, taking up the longest of the three.

"That's a short jointer," said Jim Alburgh.

"You are rather old-fashioned as well as myself. We call it, in modern times, simply a jointer. When I was a boy, we had a long and a short jointer; but the former is seldom seen in a shop at the present time. This jointer is twenty-two inches long, and they are made up to thirty inches. The long jointer was three feet and a half and even four feet long. Have you any idea what the use of this plane is?"

"It is used in making joints," answered Thad at a venture.

"Not very definite. Carpenters are sometimes called joiners, and the reason is plain enough. If you were going to lay a floor, it would be necessary to joint the edges of the boards; and this plane would be used for that purpose. In a word, the jointer is needed to get a straight edge on pieces of wood more than a foot or two in length. If two boards are exactly straight on the edges, they will make a good job.

"Here is the last plane we shall consider now. It is the shortest of the four, and it is made of steel or iron. It is called a block-plane, and can be used only in planing across the grain of the wood. When you have sawed off a piece of work, this plane would be used to smooth off the end of the wood. It is quite different from the others. The first three have double irons, while this one has only a single iron."

Mr. Brookbine took up the block-plane, and removed the iron from it. "This is called the iron, though it is always made of the best of steel," he continued. "The slant made by grinding off the end of the iron, so it will be sharp, is called the bevel. In the first three planes, the bevel is on the under side when the implement is used. In the block-plane, the bevel is on the upper side."

"But what are the double irons for in the other planes?" asked Thad. "I have seen them, but I never knew what the extra one was for."

"That is a sensible question, Thad. If the grain of the wood were always straight, — that is, parallel with the length of the board, — a single iron would answer very well. But wood, like some men and women, is sometimes cross-grained. The tendency of the iron in the plane is to follow the grain as far as the face of the plane will permit. The edge of the upper iron is curved a little, so that it prevents the cutter from going in too deep; and it turns the shaving up in such a manner that it don't choke up the opening. The upper iron also stiffens the lower one, which is now made very thin compared with the custom made years ago.

"I judge that some of you have used a plane, or tried to do so. If so, you have found great difficulty in getting your tool set right. These planes are of the latest pattern. In old planes the iron is set with a wooden wedge. You have to drive in the wedge with a hammer; and, when you take it out, you have to strike several smart blows on the top or the back end. To get the iron just right bothers the beginner more than any thing else.

"In these planes there are no wedges. A little lever is moved, and the iron is fast; as you may see by trying it. Under the iron you notice a screw, which may be turned by the thumb without taking the hand from the plane. By turning this screw to the left, you force the iron down so that it cuts a thicker shaving. Turn it to the right, and you get a thinner shaving. You have no use for a hammer, unless it be to knock the iron to one side or the other; for the edge of the cutter must be exactly parallel to the surface of the plane. That will do for planes. — What next, Dory?"

A patent bitstock, very beautifully made, with the metal parts nickel-plated, was handed to the carpenter. The boys knew what it was, though most of them had never seen one of that kind.

"This is sometimes called a brace, though bit-stock is the more common name in this country. It has some peculiarities, — the first, that the socket will hold a bit of any common shape, the

SOMETHING ABOUT TOOLS AND WORK. 251

holder adapting itself to the form as it is screwed up.

"The second is a ratchet-arrangement, by which a hole may be bored close to a partition. With an ordinary bitstock, you cannot bore a hole within three inches of a wall, or any other fixed body. After adjusting the ratchet, you may turn the crank half around, or as far as you can; then you can carry the crank back without turning the bit, and repeat the movement as long as may be necessary."

Dory next handed up a large bundle of bits. "This is an augur-bit," the carpenter continued, holding up one of this kind. "This is a pod-bit, and this a centre-bit. Here is a reamer, used to enlarge a hole in a piece of metal, as a hinge. This is a countersink, to fit the opening of a hole in wood or iron to the head of a screw.

"This is an iron square, to be used mainly in heavy work, such as framing a house. These are try-squares, very handy for bench-work. This is a bevel, with which you get the slant of any thing, and reproduce it in your work. Here is a package of two-foot rules. I shall give one to each of you, for a mechanic should always have his rule about him. Carry it in your pocket. A level: in putting up a shelf, for example, you will ascertain when the board is horizontal by applying this implement."

Many other tools were taken from the box, but the master-carpenter's method of describing such things has been sufficiently shown.

"Now, my lads, the next thing is to dispose these tools where you can get at them," Mr. Brookbine proceeded. "We have six benches, and more will be put up when they are needed. Each of them is provided with a bench-hook and a wooden vise, or bench-screw."

"What is a bench-hook?" asked Phil Gawner.

"This iron with half a dozen teeth like a saw. Under it is a lever, so that it may be raised or lowered, according to the thickness of the board you are planing, which it holds in place. Behind each bench we shall put a shelf, on which the planes are to be kept."

"Can't we keep them on the bench, as most carpenters do?" asked Dory.

"You can, but I don't think that is the best way. You see that each bench is provided with a dust-brush, to be used in removing the shavings;

and a neat workman will keep his bench as free as possible of rubbish. If you want to brush off your bench, you must move your planes twice, or put them on the floor. On the shelf they are always out of the way when not in use. We will make this shelf at once. We will have it four feet long, and six inches wide. It will be large enough to accommodate some other tools."

"Are we to make them of these old box-covers?" asked Ned Bellows.

"The shelves are to be permanent, and we will make them of new lumber. You need just twelve superficial feet of board, with a sufficient allowance for waste. The latter item is one of great importance to the carpenter; for a man may waste more lumber than would suffice to pay his wages, by being careless, or using bad judgment. We will go to the lumber-shed, and see what we can find."

Mr. Brookbine led the way. Captain Gildrock had provided a large supply of boards, plank, joist, and small stuff, which had been "stuck up" in the building provided for the purpose.

"Now, boys, see if you can find the right material for the shelves," said the carpenter. "You have your rules, and you can measure as much as you please."

The pupils fell to pulling over and measuring the boards. All of them figured up what shape the board must be to furnish what would be needed.

"I have it!" exclaimed Ben Ludlow. "Here is just the board to make the whole of them. It is just a foot wide."

"Then, it won't do," replied the carpenter. "It is neither long enough nor wide enough."

But Thad found one that was twelve feet and a half long by thirteen inches at one end and fourteen at the other. Mr. Brookbine said it would do, and it was carried to the shop.

CHAPTER XXIV.

WORK FOR THE HEAD AND THE HANDS.

THE boys were given to skylarking. Lick Milton and Phil Gawner were carrying the board. It rested on the right shoulder of one and the left shoulder of the other, with the arm above the elbow raised to keep it in place. Just before they reached the shop, Dick Short, who was half monkey in his movements, made a sudden spring, leaping upon the top of the board.

Down went the board, and down went the two boys under it. Dick turned a somerset, and came down upon his feet. Phil Gawner was not at all pleased with the incident; and, picking himself up, he rushed upon the assailant, evidently determined to thrash him for his trouble. But Dick Short had no idea of getting into a fight, and ran away as fast as his legs would carry him.

Phil chased him till they approached a tall maple whose lower limbs were at least ten feet above the ground. Dick seized hold of the tree, and went up it like a monkey. Phil attempted to grasp his feet, but the boy-ape kicked until he was out of reach of his pursuer.

"Let me get hold of you!" exclaimed Phil, rubbing his elbows, which had suffered in his fall.

"I'll let you get hold of me if you can," laughed Dick.

"What are you about here? Don't you know it is school-time?" demanded Mr. Brookbine, who was indignantly following the skylarker. "Come down out of that tree!"

"Send Phil back to the shop, and I will," replied Dick.

"Will you come down, or shall I fetch you down?" added the carpenter very decidedly.

"Fetch me down, if you please," answered Dick with a chuckle.

Possibly the runaway thought he should like to see the master-carpenter climb the tree. Captain Gildrock had come out of the shop, but he did not interfere with the instructor in mechanics. Very likely he desired to see how he would manage the case.

"Here, Tom!" said Mr. Brookbine after a whistle. He addressed the call to a tremendous

DICK SHORT UNDER GUARD. Page 257.

St. Bernard dog, which had come to Beech Hill with him.

Tom promptly obeyed the summons. His master pointed up the tree, and soon got the eyes of the canine fixed on the culprit. Then he directed him to lie down at the foot of the maple. The dog appeared to understand his mission. The principal was glad to find the carpenter did not display any thing like anger.

"Now, Phil, we will go back to the shop, and attend to those shelves," said Mr. Brookbine.

Phil wanted very much to get hold of Dick Short. He looked up at him, and then at the dog. He said nothing; for he realized that the instructor intended to punish his assailant in his own way, and he was rather curious to see what the result would be.

Phil and the rest of the boys followed the carpenter. The board was taken into the shop, and not a word said about the incident which had just occurred.

"We have no saw-horses, or trestles as some call them. But we can use a couple of these boxes, and in a few days we shall be able to make all the furniture we need in the shop," said the carpenter as pleasantly as though no breach of discipline had occurred.

The pupils expected him to say something on the subject of skylarking in general, and the late case in particular. He directed a couple of the boys to place the boxes where he wanted them, and then to put the board upon them.

"There will be waste in that board: I think the one I picked out would have done better. It was just the right length," said Ben Ludlow, who was rather displeased because his board had been rejected.

"How wide was your board, Ben?" asked the carpenter.

"Just one foot to a hair. It was exactly wide enough to make two shelves," answered Ben.

"You think you were right, Ben, and I am glad to see that you are ready to argue your side of the question. If I don't prove that you were wrong, I hope you will stick to your opinion," replied Mr. Brookbine, as he took one of the slitting-saws from the bench.

He sawed about three inches into one of the lids of the boxes. Calling Ben close to him, he applied his rule, where the sixteenths were marked, and asked the doubtful student how wide the slit was.

"Just a sixteenth, as near as I can make it out," replied Ben.

The boys began to laugh, for they saw the result of the argument.

"There will be four edges to the two strips of six inches in width, when the board is sawed through its length, will there not, Ben?"

"Yes, sir," answered the other side of the question.

"Will those edges be perfectly smooth?"

"Of course they will not: they will be just as the saw left them."

"They are not likely to be sawed perfectly straight, even if the job were done by an experienced workman. How much shall we have to plane off in order to get the edges straight and smooth?"

"I don't know, — half an inch from each, perhaps. I give it up. I was wrong, sir."

"Not half an inch, with such clear, finish-lumber as this board: that would be shameful. Call it an eighth of an inch; and from the four sides you will take off half an inch, besides the sixteenth cut out by the saw. Your shelves would be less than five and three-quarters wide, which is not six inches. When we want any stock to be of a certain width, it won't do to make it a quarter of an inch less than that. You might waste the whole board in that way."

"I give it up, and it was stupid on my part," added Ben.

"Such mistakes are to be expected from beginners. Now let us look at the board we have. In the length we have six inches to spare, which is abundant. Now let us see if the ends of the board are sound. Are there any checks or splits in it?"

None of any consequence were found.

"Now, boys, laying out the work is quite as important as doing it. If you make blunders in your calculations, the job will not come out as you expect. We must first cut the board into six lengths."

"We are to take out six-sixteenths of an inch for the saw-cuts," suggested Steve Baxter.

"Why six?"

"Because the board is to be sawed into six lengths."

"How many cuts do you make in order to get six pieces?"

"Six, sir."

"Do you think so? Look it over a little more."

The rest of the boys, or most of them, looked upon the problem as a puzzle; and they were interested in it, though none appeared to have made up their minds.

"Of course you have to cut six times to get six pieces," said Phil Gawner. "I think Steve Baxter is right."

"Let us look at it, and see. When I have made one cut with the saw, how many pieces do I get?" asked Mr. Brookbine.

"One," shouted half a dozen of the pupils.

"The second cut?"

"Two pieces."

"Right; and the third, three, and the fourth, four," continued the instructor. "When I cut the fifth time, how many have I?"

"Five!" shouted the boys triumphantly.

"But what is there left?" asked the instructor, astonished at the answer.

"The rest of the board," answered Steve Baxter.

"Isn't the rest of the board the sixth piece?" demanded the carpenter.

The students looked rather blankly at each other; and Mr. Brookbine saw that they were not convinced, simple as the problem was.

He took a stick, and cut it so that it was twenty-four inches long. Using his rule, he marked it off into pieces four inches in length. Sawing off the piece on the right of the first mark, he handed it to Steve. He asked the students to count as he cut off the lengths.

"Five!" screamed the boys when he had made the fifth cut.

"Here is the sixth piece. It is just four inches long. Now, where shall I put in the sixth cut?" asked Mr. Brookbine, as he handed the rest of the stick to Steve. "You have six pieces, though I have cut but five times."

"That's so; but I can't see why it should be so," replied Steve vacantly.

"The first four cuts each gave me one piece, or four pieces in all. The fifth cut gave me two pieces, did it not? for the rest of the board is a piece as well as the others."

All of them could see it then; and the principal applied the result to other numbers, and the students were willing to admit that an equal division into ten parts was made with nine cuts.

"It is surprising how little things bother us sometimes," continued Mr. Brookbine. "But we shall never get our shelves made at this rate. As we have leeway enough in the length of this board, we will cut the pieces four feet and one inch in length. Nat Long, you may measure it off on one side, and, Ned Bellows, you may do the same on the other side."

Both of them made mistakes, which were detected by the others; but at last the board was marked off into equal lengths. The same boys were required to take the steel square, and rule off the lengths. They were not inclined to do it accurately, as the instructor insisted they should. The cutting-off saws were then given to a couple of the boys.

"You must not saw on the mark, but at the right-hand side of it, and close to it. Hold on! you are a quarter of an inch off the mark, Tom Ridley. That won't do! You must cut the board at just the thickness of the saw-blade from the mark, so that you can see it all the time. When the sawdust covers it, blow it off."

"But I can't make the saw start where I want it to," replied Tom.

"Catch hold of the board with your hand, and let the end of your thumb rest against the saw-blade to keep it in place," replied the carpenter, taking another saw, and showing the pupils how to do it. "That's it! Now you have got a start. Put three fingers through the handle, and keep the forefinger out straight, and pressed against it. Let the saw run lightly; don't bear on, but rather lift up at the start. When you bear on at all, do it on the downward stroke."

"I am running away from the mark," said Corny Minkfield, at the other end of the board.

"Don't do it: saw close to the mark all the way. Don't grasp the handle of the saw so tightly. Hold it rather loosely, and take as long strokes as you can," interposed Mr. Brookbine, as he applied a small try-square to the angle made by the saw-blade and the board. "Your cut through the board is not plumb."

The five cuts were finally made, and they had six pieces about four feet and an inch long. An opportunity had been given to all the class to try the saw, and some of them did very well.

"Now, we want a little calculation again in regard to the width of the board. The time spent in making sure that you are right before you cut is never wasted. This piece of lumber is thirteen inches wide at the narrow end. We will cut each of these boards into two pieces lengthwise. But we will first reduce each to a uniform width of thirteen inches."

In the course of half an hour all this was done, and the six shelves were ready to go upon the bench.

CHAPTER XXV.

THE SECOND CLASS AT THE CARPENTER'S BENCH.

MR. BROOKBINE directed one piece of the board to be taken to each of the benches. He then stationed two of the class at a bench, intimating they were to work together, and divide the labor. When not actually employed, either one of the couple was to observe the other; but he was not to criticise him, for this might lead to quarrels. Every one could improve by noticing the mistakes of others.

"The first thing is to get one straight and square edge on each board," said the carpenter. "You will put one end of the board in the vise, and place one of the pins in the front of the bench, so that it will support the other end."

One of each pair of workmen adjusted the vise, while the other put the pin in the right place. The edge of the board was to be parallel with the top of the bench, and several of the boys had to make changes in its position. The instructor found it necessary to number the benches, and then to designate the workmen at each as No. 1 and No. 2.

"Now, No. 2 will take the fore-plane. Place the end of it on the bench, and hold it so that you can sight along the face. Put the fingers of your left hand on the screw under the iron. Now turn the screw till the edge of the cutter is just a very little below the face."

Of course, half the students turned the wrong way; and it required some time to adjust the iron. The carpenter explained again that the screw must be turned towards the left to send the cutter down. At last the boys were all ready.

"Probably not many of you have got it just right. I want you to take off a very thin shaving at first. After one stroke with the plane, you will see how to alter it," continued the instructor, as the boys made their first attempt. Some of the planes took off no shaving at all, and some dug deep into the wood.

"What do you call a thin shaving, Mr. Brookbine?" asked Jim Alburgh.

"One not thicker than a piece of ordinary writing-paper to begin with. By and by you can take a thick shaving, when you have learned how. We must feel our way, and not spoil the board," replied the carpenter, as he walked along by the boys, and looked at each plane.

After a second or third stroke of the tool, the shaving was right all along the line. The workmen were required to plane till they had a smooth surface. Some of them were nicer and more particular than others, and the latter were told to do theirs over again. This discipline soon made them all careful.

"Now, lift the end of the board, and sight along the edge of it," said Mr. Brookbine, doing as he described with the board nearest to him. "This piece slants, or bevels, on the edge; and very likely all the rest of them have the same fault."

"Mine does," added Phil Gawner. "I could slide down hill on it."

"Is that what the squinting is for?" asked Tom Ridley. "I have often seen carpenters do it."

"That is what it is for. You are to educate your eye so that you can tell at a glance whether a piece of work is straight, or not. I dare say, you can't tell now whether the edge of the board is true, or not," added Mr. Brookbine, as he passed along the benches, and examined the work of each boy.

"Not a single one is right," continued he. "As is apt to be the case with beginners, you all lean your plane to the right, just as you do with the saw. Most of you have got it so far out of the way that you can't help seeing it with your eye."

The students admitted that they could see it. The carpenter told them to try again, and be sure to keep the plane perfectly level on the edge of the board. He directed them to take hold of the tool with the left hand, so that the middle finger would touch the perpendicular part of the board. After they had taken a few strokes more, they were told to sight their work again. Several of them declared that it was right now. Two of them had to use the plane again.

"Take the small try-square, each of you. Place the handle against the perpendicular of the board, and the blade across the edge." The carpenter took one of the squares, and showed them how to do it. "If you have it nearly square, it will do for our present purpose. Now take the jointer. Be sure that the cutter strikes the board at the end where you begin. Put the left hand on the plane as before, and be sure that you keep the jointer perfectly level."

The boys made the first stroke with the long plane. The carpenter had set the irons so that they took off a very thin shaving.

"Mine will cut only in the middle," said Tom Ridley.

"Mine will take hold only at the ends," added Ben Ludlow.

"That's all right," replied the instructor. "Some of you have gouged out the middle of the board, and others have taken off the ends, with the fore-plane. The jointer is long enough to correct all these faults; only don't lean the plane over either way."

After a few strokes the pupils were required to sight along their work. Under the constant admonitions of the carpenter, the edge was so nearly square that they could detect no fault. They were told to use the square. This trial proved that not one was exactly square. The plane was used again.

When the boys had satisfied themselves, Mr. Brookbine inspected the work, and was able to find something out of the way with every piece. But at last the boards were all right. The students were required to measure the width of the pieces in the narrowest place. They varied considerably, but all had over a quarter of an inch to spare.

"Now we will use a new tool, that I have not mentioned," continued the carpenter, taking a bundle of gauges from one of the boxes, and putting one on each bench. "Take your rule, and set this gauge at just six inches." He showed them how to do it, and then looked at each one to see that it was right.

After telling the class to do as he did, he placed one end of the board against the bench-hook, and ran the gauge the entire length of it. Turning it over, but still keeping the straight edge on the right, he gauged the other side. Hardly one of the boys succeeded in carrying the gauge the whole length of the board. It slipped out of place because it was not held right. But at last all the pieces were gauged on both sides.

"Now we are to plane the other edge of the board down to the gauge-mark. As you are to plane down about a quarter of an inch, you can take off a thicker shaving. You must keep watch of the mark, for you are not to go the breadth of a hair below it."

The pupils were exceedingly cautious, and after every shaving they looked at the mark. When they were pretty near it, the carpenter told them to take the jointer. All of them applied the try-square, correcting the faults as they discovered them; and they made very good progress. They were directed to plane out the gauge-mark, which they could see on the planed surface. Mr. Brookbine kept inspecting the work until it was satisfactory to him.

"Now, we want to make these shelves four feet long,—just four feet, not a little more or a little less. Lay the board flat on the bench, and take the larger try-square, for the blade of the small one is only four inches and a half long. We will now square one of the ends of the shelf, but we don't want to take off more than a quarter of an inch. In marking this, the lead-pencil won't do, and you must use the point of your pocket-knife."

The carpenter saw that it was done properly. Then each pupil was required to take the larger of the two back-saws, and cut off the board on the mark. In using this saw, they were to touch very lightly, rather lifting it up than bearing on with it.

After the utmost watchfulness on the part of the instructor, the cut was passably well done. Most of the workmen had used the small square in their efforts to keep the saw at right angles with the face of the board. Of course, there were some twists in the cut; and half of them had made the end slightly bevelling, in spite of all their efforts to avoid this fault.

"It is very well for beginners. You can only do this thing off-hand after considerable practice, and I don't think any six apprentices ever did any better than you have. Now put the end you have just cut off into the vise, so that you can smooth off the work with the block-plane. With this tool you can correct the error of the saw, and take out the bevel. Use the square constantly, both along the width and thickness of the shelf. The chances are, that you will take off too much if you are not very careful."

Most of the block-planes cut too rankly, and it was some time before they were properly adjusted. The boys were very careful, for each one felt that it would be a disaster to spoil the board. When the end was made smooth and square, Captain Gildrock passed along the benches, and he was generous of his praise. The students were encouraged.

"Now measure off four feet from the square end, and use your pocket-knife to mark with. You must learn to do this accurately, and there must not be the variation of a shaving in the length of the shelves."

After the students had measured the boards, the carpenter went over all of them. Only two were inaccurate, and the instructor showed the delinquents where their fault was. The larger square was then called for.

"Put the point of your knife on the mark you have made to indicate four feet, and bring the blade of the square against it. See that the handle is against the wood. Press down the square, so that it will not slip while you are ruling it off. Hold it tight all the time. Now mark it. When we want to be very correct, we use a knife to mark with, because the line thus made has no essential thickness.

"Very well," continued Mr. Brookbine, after he had inspected the marking. "We are to saw the end off outside of this line. We must keep the saw against the mark, but not cut it out. Remember that you have no leeway, — at least, only the thickness of the mark, which you will use up in smoothing off this end of the board."

The students sawed the end off with the utmost caution, using the square to keep the tool plumb. Mr. Brookbine pronounced it well done. With the experience they had obtained with the block-plane, they smoothed off the end without any difficulty; and the boards were ready for the next operation.

"Now we must round off the outside corners of the shelf," said the carpenter. "At this point you need a little geometry, and this is where the high-school comes in. This board is six inches wide. Rule off six inches from the length at each end. What sort of a figure will that make?"

"This class never studied geometry," interposed Captain Gildrock.

"But they know this figure," replied the carpenter.

"It is a square," said Thad Glovering.

"Right. The diagonal of a square is a line connecting the opposite corners: rule in a diagonal.

Now rule another from the other corners. I dare say Mr. Bentnick will not find my geometry as scientific as his own. Where the diagonals cross each other is the centre of the square. Take the compasses, and set the points three inches apart. The problem is to inscribe a circle inside of a square, though it is necessary to mark only a quarter of the square."

The quarter of a circle was inscribed, and formed the round corner of the shelf. It was repeated on the other end.

CHAPTER XXVI.

THE END OF THE FIRST SCHOOL-DAY AT BEECH HILL.

THE next operation for the class was to round off the ends of the shelves. Mr. Brookbine asked the boys how they would do it. One said he would plane it off, another would saw it off, and a third would chop it off with the hatchet.

"There are three ways, neither of which is practicable," continued the carpenter. "You can't plane off a circular face, and the saw or the hatchet would leave the work in a rough state. We will use all three of the methods named. First we will saw off the corner; then we will cut away a little more with the hatchet or shave; and finally we will plane it off smoothly, though we shall not use a plane, but another tool for the purpose. Mark off the part you will saw from the board, and saw it off."

This was done without any aid from the teacher.

Then shingling-hatchets were used to take off the two corners left by the saw.

"Now we will introduce you to the spokeshave, an exceedingly useful tool for many purposes. It does the same work as a plane, and in the same manner; but as it has no appreciable length, compared with a plane, we can follow curves with it. Put the corner of the board in the vise, and then with the spokeshave work down to the circular line. Don't cut the mark off; never do that. It will take you some time to do this job."

Mr. Brookbine showed the workmen how to use the new tool; and they went to work with it in earnest, being greatly interested in their occupation. While they were thus engaged, the carpenter went to the door to ascertain the state of things at the tree where one of the class was taking a vacation. Tom lay at the foot of the tree, and Dick Short was seated on a limb twenty feet from the ground. If the prisoner moved, the dog looked up at him; and Dick could think of no strategy by which he could outwit the faithful sentinel. The instructor only looked, and then returned to the bench. Dick was likely to stay where he was until the St. Bernard changed his quarters.

"Use the try-square when you get near the mark," said the carpenter, as he resumed his place. "Every part of the quarter circle must be true."

One after another the students carried the shelf to Mr. Brookbine, as they finished it. Some criticisms were made on the work, and some of it had to be corrected. In due time they were all completed and approved. The sides of the shelves were just as they came from the planing-machine; and the boys were directed to lay them on the bench, and use the smoothing-plane upon them. These planes were adjusted so they cut the thinnest possible shaving. The shelves were made as smooth as glass.

"I don't see how we are to put the shelves up," said Ben Ludlow when the boards were finished.

"That is just the river we are to cross next," replied Mr. Brookbine. "I believe we have no iron brackets, though I dare say the machinists at the other end of the shop could make them for us if we are willing to wait for them. For the want of them we will make a couple of ogee brackets of pine for each shelf."

"Ogee!" exclaimed Steve Baxter. "Is that Latin?"

"It may be: I don't know. My Greek and Latin were neglected. The ogee form is very common, and there is an ogee arch in architecture. — We need a blackboard in the shop as well as in the schoolroom," said the carpenter, turning to Captain Gildrock. "But I can chalk it out on one of these box-tops."

He made a drawing of half a square, connecting the ends of the two sides by a diagonal. In other words, it was a right-angled triangle, resting on one of the points, with the side perpendicular to the top.

"This is the shape of the board we shall get out. I divide the diagonal into two equal lengths. Each half will be the chord of the arc of a circle. The upper arc is outside of the chord, and the lower one inside of the chord;" and Mr. Brookbine drew the arcs with his chalk.

"But you can't get that figure out of that piece of board," interposed Thad, who was thinking with all his might.

"Very true, my lad; and I am glad to see that you have your eyes open. I want you to correct all my blunders. In order to get the ogee out of this piece of wood, I must draw a line parallel to the diagonal, far enough inside of it to permit me to get the arc out of the piece."

"Isn't there any other way to do it?" asked Dory.

"There is another way, and perhaps it is a better one," replied Mr. Brookbine, as he drew another square on the board. "On the diagonal I draw the two arcs" (suiting the action to the words). "With a keyhole-saw, I follow this curved line, and cut the board in two pieces. Perhaps this will be the better way to do it, as it will give a little different practice."

"That is the way I was thinking of," added Dory.

"I am glad you thought of it. You and Thad may go to the lumber-room, and get the board to make these brackets of. We want six pairs of them, and we are to get out six pieces six inches square."

The boys soon returned with a board about twenty inches long and a little over a foot wide. It was sawed into six pieces, planed and squared to the exact size required. While the boys were thus employed, the carpenter made a pattern of a single bracket out of a piece of quarter-inch board. As soon as one of the square boards was ready, he applied the pattern to it, and marked the ogee line with a sharp-pointed pencil.

The instructor then distributed the keyhole-saws, and explained how to use them. The square boards were put into the vises, after they had been marked from the pattern. The saws were narrowest near the points. If the pupils found any difficulty in turning the saw, they were required to take short strokes, using the tip end, until they got over the difficulty. The narrower the saw, the more easily it could be turned from a straight line.

"Turn the bottom piece up-side-down, and it will exactly correspond with the upper piece, if you have sawed all the way on the line," said the carpenter, when some of the boys had finished the first piece.

"Mine don't," added Lick Milton. "I kept close to the line all the way."

"Another blunder of mine!" exclaimed Mr. Brookbine, "for which I tender my apology. I told you to saw on the right of the mark. This is always to be done when practicable; but I neglected to say that it is not always convenient, or even possible, to do it in that way. In this instance the line ought to have been sawed out, and then the cut would have been precisely in the middle of the piece. Sometimes, too, when you cannot shift the work end to end, it becomes necessary to saw on the left of the line. In cutting the next one, saw out the line, and see how it comes out then."

The result verified the statement of the teacher, for the two pieces almost coincided. The workmen were directed to apply the spokeshave to the curves on the bracket, and they were soon ready.

"Now we will proceed to put the shelves up," continued Mr. Brookbine.

"Not this afternoon," interposed Captain Gildrock. "It is four o'clock now, and we must be as punctual in closing the sessions of the school as in beginning them. I must say, my lads, that I have been very much pleased with your attention and general good conduct on the first day of the Beech-Hill Industrial School."

"For one, I should like to go on with the work until supper-time," said Ben Ludlow.

"So would I!" shouted about all the rest of them.

"I think not, boys," replied the captain. "I am glad to find you so much interested in your work, but we must not overdo it. We shall keep to our regular hours. The rest of the day, and the morning until nine o'clock, belongs to you; but you must not forget the lessons assigned to you for to-morrow. You may use the boats for a couple of hours now, if you choose. There are enough of the small craft to accommodate the whole school."

The boys put on their coats, and left the shop. Some of them were curious to know what had become of Dick Short, and they walked to the maple-tree. But Mr. Brookbine ordered them off, saying that they were to have no communication with Dick. Tom still kept his position at the foot of the tree.

"Mr. Brookbine," called Dick, when he saw the instructor come out of the shop.

"Well, my lad, what is it?" asked the carpenter. "Do you want to jump on another board, and kill a couple more boys?"

"I haven't killed any boys," replied Dick.

"If you haven't, it isn't your fault. You went to work in the right way to do it, or, at least, to hurt them badly. What do you want now?"

"Don't you think I have been up this tree about long enough, Mr. Brookbine?" continued Dick in the meekest of tones.

"I don't know: you know better than I do. If you haven't been up there long enough to keep you from skylarking in school-hours, you had better stay there a week or two longer; and Tom will see that you don't come down."

"I will be as sober as a judge in school-hours after this. I didn't think what I was about when I jumped on that board, and I am sorry I did it," pleaded Dick, who was heartily disgusted with being watched by the big dog.

"Very well: I am satisfied; but I don't know whether Phil Gawner is, or not," added the instructor.

"I will beg his pardon, or let him thrash me, just as he chooses," suggested Dick.

The instructor called Phil as he was going down to the lake. As soon as Phil came within hailing-distance of the tree, Dick made his apology, which was promptly accepted; and the culprit was permitted to descend the tree. His punishment was so odd that it puzzled him. He had often been whipped in school for his pranks; but to be imprisoned over two hours up in a tree, with a dog to keep guard over him, was more than he could stand.

Most of the students were at the lake by this time. Dory had already invited Oscar Chester to take a sail in the Goldwing, and he had accepted. The four members of the Goldwing Club had been in the schooner so much that they preferred to take a four-oar boat that was moored on the lake.

In fifteen minutes the Goldwing was out on Lake Champlain. The wind was fresh from the south-west, and the lake is not the best place in the world for a sailboat. Puffs of wind, and even pretty smart squalls, sometimes come from the hills that surround this beautiful sheet of water, so that the skipper has to be on the alert.

"I should be very glad to have you steer her now, Oscar, if you wish," said Dory to his passenger as soon as the boat was well out in the lake.

"Thank you, Dory," replied Oscar. "I think we shall be the best of friends, after all."

"It will not be my fault if we are not," added Dory.

Just then the Monkey, which Sim Green had brought up from Burlington on Saturday, came out off the river in charge of Bolingbroke Millweed.

CHAPTER XXVII.

OSCAR CHESTER TAKES A LESSON IN BOATING.

"I DON'T know why it is, but every fellow I ever knew took to boats," said Oscar Chester, who had just gone to the helm of the Goldwing. "The fellows here are just like all the rest of them, and about every one of them is in the boats. There come three rowboats out of the river."

"In Burlington all the boys were anxious to get out on the lake. I was like all the rest of them; and, as my father was a pilot on a steamer, I had a better chance than most of them. There is the Goldwing Club," added Dory, as the four-oar boat came out of the river.

"What's the Goldwing Club?" asked Oscar.

"We used to have a flat-bottom boat in Burlington, and we formed a club. The craft was smashed; and, after I bought the Goldwing, we used to sail in her. We learned to row, but the club are not doing very well with their oars," added Dory, as one of the party "caught a crab."

"Who is managing that sailboat, Dory?" asked Oscar, as he pointed at the Monkey.

"Bolly Millweed; but he don't know how to do it, and he ought not to come out on the lake without a skipper."

"That's just my case, but I am very anxious to learn how to do it."

"You will soon learn. One sails a boat as he drives a horse: it is done more by the feeling than by the sight. All you need is practice, for the science is very simple. But I think we had better come about, for I am afraid some of those fellows will get into trouble. Bolly has trimmed his sail in a very careless manner; and, if a puff of wind should come upon him, he don't know what to do any more than a baby. His sheet is made fast too."

"I don't know any better than he does what to do."

"Bolly has the wind on the beam, but he has his sail trimmed to go as close to the wind as his boat will lie. Now put the helm down, if you please, and we will come about."

"Which way is 'down'?" asked Oscar blankly. "Do you mean down the lake?"

"It happens to be so in this instance, but that is not what we mean by 'down.' 'Down' is to leeward. 'Up' is the way from which the wind comes, and 'down' the way towards which it blows."

"Nothing was said about 'up' and 'down' on the steamer the other day."

"In a steamer it makes no difference which way the wind blows, and the terms don't mean any thing in particular. But, in a sailboat, we manage her altogether by the wind. Now put the helm down," added Dory, as he stood by the sheets.

Oscar did as he was directed; and, as soon as he shifted the tiller, all the sails began to shake.

"There is some mistake about that," said Oscar, as he began to restore the tiller to its former position. "That knocks all the wind out of the sails."

"You did just right! keep the helm down!" exclaimed Dory with energy. "She is doing just as she should."

"But I don't see how you are going to sail with the canvas flapping like this," added Oscar, as he put the helm hard down again.

"She is in stays now. Wait a moment, and you will see what she does," replied Dory.

At that instant the wind caught the jib, and the schooner began to swing very rapidly. The other sails filled at the same time.

"Now right the helm and meet her," continued Dory. "Be lively about it. Carry the tiller over till you feel a strong resistance. Over with it, before she falls off too far."

Oscar obeyed, but he had been hardly prompt enough in his movements. The sails were brought too nearly at right angles with the wind, which caused her to careen till the new skipper's nerves were badly shaken. A bucket of water poured in over the wash-board.

"Down with the helm, Oscar!" said Dory sharply. "The other way!" he added, springing to the tiller, and putting it hard down.

"You said 'down' was the other way," retorted Oscar in a tone that indicated anger on his part.

"Now we are all right," said Dory, laughing, as the boat came up so that the pressure was eased off the sails.

"'Down' can't be both ways," growled Oscar.

"But sometimes it is one side of the boat, and sometimes the other," replied Dory very gently, for he saw that a storm was gathering in the breast of his companion. "Sometimes it is port, and sometimes it is starboard."

"I don't see how any one is to know which way is 'down,'" muttered Oscar.

"I can tell which is 'down' every time, and without fail; and so can you, after you have sailed a boat a little longer. 'Up' is the way the wind comes from, and 'down' is the other way. Before you tacked, you had the wind on the port side of you, and 'down' was to starboard. Now you have the wind on the starboard, and 'down' is on the port side."

"I don't think I understand it very well, and you had better take the helm. I am afraid I shall upset her," said Oscar, somewhat disgusted with his experience so far.

"I think the wind is rather too fresh for a first lesson to-day," replied Dory, as he took the tiller. "It would be better for you to try it when there isn't wind enough to upset her if you make a mistake. You must excuse me if I spoke too quick to you just now, for the Goldwing would have gone over in another second if she had had her own way."

"I was just beginning to get a little mad," replied Oscar. "It don't take much of a breeze to put me into a passion. But it is all right now, and I won't get mad if I can help it. It comes upon me before I know it. Do you think I shall ever be able to sail a boat?"

"I know you will. I will tack the boat several times, so that you can see just how it is done. I suppose you know how to drive a horse, Oscar?"

"Of course I do."

"If you let your horse run off a steep bank, you will upset the carriage. A boat won't do it a bit better. If you let the wind blow square against the sails, she won't go ahead; and there is nothing under the canopy to prevent her from going over, even with less wind than there is to-day. You should never let her get into such a pickle, any more than you would drive your horse off a precipice."

"I can see what you mean. There is nothing to prevent her from tipping over."

"On the wind, as the Goldwing is now, we keep her so that the sails will fill. Just a little movement of the tiller will spill them all: see if it don't," continued Dory, as he put the helm down a very little. "All the sails are shaking. I keep her so that she bears on the helm all the time. When the pressure is too little, I know that she is coming up into the wind, and I shift the tiller."

"I begin to see through it."

When he had a good full, Dory put the helm down, explaining his action. When the jib began to draw, he began to right the helm. Oscar got the idea; and, after a few more tacks, he understood it perfectly, and was permitted to do it himself.

"Suppose you get caught with the wind blowing square against the sails, and are in danger of going over, what do you do — put the helm down?" asked Oscar.

"If the wind was fresh I should not wait for her to come up, for she might go over before she came up to a safe position. Let me take the helm again, and I will show you."

The skipper put the helm up, and in a moment the water began to pour in over the wash-board. Oscar thought she was going over, and he convulsively grasped the seat with both hands. Dory gave the end of the fore and main sheets a twitch, in the twinkling of an eye, which cast them off. The two principal sails ran out instantly, the pressure was removed, and the boat came up to an even keel.

"That is the way to save yourself when you get into a tight place, Oscar; but you ought never to get into such a tight place as that. A boat can't possibly upset unless she is in that position. But, before she falls off enough to put you into chancery in that style, she will bear very hard on the tiller, which will give you warning enough. If you let go the tiller, she will come into the wind herself. The Goldwing, or any boat properly rigged and ballasted, would never get you into such a scrape: you must force her into the dangerous position. Now you may take the helm."

In half an hour Oscar could beat to windward as well as an old salt, though his education as a boatman was by no means completed. The Monkey, which had been moving at the rate of less than a mile an hour, had by this time got out into the middle of the lake, where she felt the full force of the wind.

Like all monkeys, the sloop was behaving very badly indeed; but it was solely because she was badly handled. Dory was confident she would meet with an accident; and he required Oscar to come about off Scotch Bonnet, about three miles below the mouth of the river. After some manœuvring, he got the foresail on the port side, with the mainsail on the starboard; and the Goldwing began to fly, wing-and-wing, before the wind.

The wind had a reach of several miles from the head of North-west Bay, and there was considerable sea. The schooner rolled, pitched, plunged, and yawed about at a fearful rate. Oscar found that he had his hands more than full. He wanted to give it up, but the skipper assured him he was doing as well as any one could; that all vessels knocked about like that when running exactly before a fresh wind.

"But isn't there any danger in staving along like this, Dory?" asked Oscar.

"None at all if the boat is well handled. If you vary your present course too much, one or the other of the sails would bang over to the other side. It would do no harm even then, unless it was the mainsail, and the boom hit you on the head.

"Then, if you should let her come a quarter way around, you would have her in that ugly position with the wind at right angles with the sails, and she would upset. With as much wind as there is to-day, she will go over every time you put her into chancery; and it won't be her fault either."

Oscar soon got used to the motion and the erratic gyrations of the boat, and then he enjoyed it. He had been told to steer for a tree on a hill, and he kept the course remarkably well for a beginner. The Goldwing had gone two miles in a little over ten minutes, and the shoal-water of Field's Bay was ahead of her.

"We must haul up a little, or we shall get aground," said Dory. "As we are going squarely before the wind, there is no up or down about it; and you must put the helm to starboard. But we will do it without making any sensation," he added, as he cast off the main-sheet. "The foresail will pop over to the other side, and do it with a rush. Now, starboard, very slowly."

Dory let out the main-sheet, so that the sail did not draw full. Over went the foresail with a rush.

"Steady! That is, keep her as she is." Relieved of a portion of the pressure on the mainsail, she did not heel over much under the shock. Dory was about to ask Oscar how he would come about, when a tremendous yell came up the lake from the other students.

CHAPTER XXVIII.

THE UPSETTING OF THE MONKEY, AND ITS LESSON.

"THE Monkey has upset!" exclaimed Dory, considerably excited by the catastrophe.

"You had better take the helm, Dory, for we can't wait to make any mistakes," added Oscar, as he gave the tiller to the skipper.

"Bolly is determined to drown himself, and he will do it if he keeps on trying. I did not think he had pluck enough to go out in a sailboat again without a skipper."

"But the rowboats are all around him, and they are all pulling towards the Monkey," continued Oscar. "But that sailboat don't sink, as you say the other did."

"Perhaps she has not ballast enough to carry her down. She is lying flat on her side, and the fellows that were in her are clinging to her. They are safe for a while if they will only hold on," said the skipper of the Goldwing when he had taken in the situation.

The Goldwing was within five hundred feet of the Monkey when the latter went over; and, before any of the rowboats reached the wreck, the schooner was alongside of her. The skipper had taken in the foresail; and, as she rounded-to, Oscar let go the jib-halyard, and Dory lowered the mainsail. With the boat-hook Oscar got hold of the wreck, and the schooner was hauled alongside.

Bolly, Steve Baxter, and Phil Gawner were helped into the Goldwing. All three of them were thoroughly frightened, but were not otherwise damaged.

"Who was the skipper of this boat?" asked Dory.

"Bolly; and he said he knew how to sail a boat, or we should not have come out with him," replied Phil.

"Can you skipper a boat, Bolly?" said Dory, turning to Bolly.

"I thought I could," answered Bolly sheepishly.

"You thought so last Friday, when you let that steam-launch run into you."

"But since that I have watched you, and I was sure I could do it," pleaded Bolly.

"I don't think you know any more about it now

than you did then. I told Oscar you would upset the boat when I first saw her come out of the river. I don't believe you will ever be hanged. If you are going to keep doing this thing, you had better learn to swim," added the skipper of the Goldwing.

"I won't try it again: there is something about sailing a boat that I don't understand," replied Bolly.

"A good deal that you don't understand; and, if you want to commit suicide, you had better keep on sailing a boat. You will finish the job one of these days. It is lucky this boat did not sink, like the other. If she had, some of you might have been drowned. As it is, we must get her up, and bail her out."

"If you will tell us how, we will do all the work," added Bolly.

By this time the four-oar boat came up. Corny Minkfield was acting as coxswain, in the absence of Dory. Dick Short was not in the boat, and Dave Windsor and John Brattle pulled the two after-oars.

"Where is Dick Short?" asked Dory.

"Mr. Brookbine would not let him come. He

said he must learn the lesson he lost while he was up a tree," replied Corny. "We have got two greenhorns in the boat, and we can't row worth a cent."

"No need of telling of it, for any one could see it a mile off," laughed Dory.

"Corny wants to do all the ordering while we do all the work," added Dave Windsor. "When he is appointed boss we will mind him."

"Just as you like. There is Captain Gildrock on the point watching us, and I don't believe he will let any of you fellows out in a boat again till you learn how to handle one. But we must put the Monkey in shape, and take her up the river: Sim Green don't want to lose another boat just yet."

Dory fastened a line to the mast-head of the Monkey. As the boat had gone over on the port side, he moved the Goldwing to the opposite side. But pulling on this line would only move the boat in the water without righting her.

Making another line fast to the middle of the inside of the wreck, he passed it over the side out of the water, and then drew it under the keel, carrying the rope out beyond the mast-head. The end of the line was then made fast to the stern of Corny's boat, whose crew were directed to pull with all their might when the word was given.

Dory then climbed to the foremast-head of the Goldwing, with the other line tied around his body. From this elevated position he could pull up from the fallen mast of the Monkey. He gave the word to Corny to pull, and the boat yanked away at the line; but the crew pulled so badly that they did not exert any great force.

The skipper passed his line over the spring-stay of the schooner, so that Oscar could keep what he got. When he pulled at the rope, greatly to his delight, and somewhat to his astonishment, the mast of the wreck began to rise, and the hull began to right. After it had been elevated a few feet, it was easy work; and the Monkey was soon right side up. The rowers gave a smart cheer when the work was accomplished.

Bolly and his companions timidly returned to the Monkey. All the buckets and dippers that both boats contained were in demand, and she was soon free of water. The lines were cast off, and both sailboats were ready to return to Beech Lake. Phil and John Brattle positively refused to sail with Bolly again, and the late skipper of the Monkey had his doubts about attempting to get the boat into the river without upsetting her.

"I can do it," suggested Oscar.

"I have no doubt you can, Oscar, and you may do it," replied Dory. "You will have the wind fair all the way."

Oscar took his place in the Monkey, which he soon found was not such a craft as the Goldwing. He trimmed the sail, and got under way without making any mistakes. He had the wind on the beam, and he let out the sheet of the sloop until the sail would just draw full. The craft made double the speed she had attained at any time since she came out with her incompetent skipper.

Dory followed her in the Goldwing when he got his sails up. He watched the work of his pupil with close attention as he passed the Monkey, and shouted his approval to Oscar. When he reached the point, Captain Gildrock made a signal that he would like to be taken on board the schooner; and Dory made a landing.

"No more boating for these boys at present," said the principal, as he stepped into the Goldwing. "They can neither sail a boat nor row one. Who is sailing that boat now, Dory? He is doing better than has been done with her before this afternoon."

"Oscar Chester is in charge of her. He has been sailing with me in the schooner; and, as far as he has gone, he knows how to do it," replied Dory.

"It will be impossible to keep them out of the boats; and the pupils must be taught at once how to row, and how to handle a sailboat," continued the captain, as he glanced at the rowing of the party in the four-oar boat. "When I saw that sloop-boat go over, I thought that the first day of our school was to end in a disaster. I am thankful that no one lost his life. But no one shall go out of Beech Lake again in a sailboat unless there is a skipper on board."

Dick Short welcomed the boys back to the school-grounds. He had made up the lost lesson, and was as good-natured as though he had not been punished. Before breakfast the next morning, the boys all walked over to the beach in the little lake, and went into the water. In the evening a great deal had been said about learning to swim. It was found that only eight boys out of the twenty-two could swim a stroke. Dory and Harry Franklin were appointed instructors in this department; and they were to have a lesson every day, when the weather was suitable.

Some pieces of plank were obtained at the lumber-shed, and conveyed to the beach. Holding these floats with their hands, some of the boys ventured out into deep water. The first thing was to obtain the necessary confidence. They were told how to move their feet in the operation, and the first trials were very satisfactory.

The schoolroom exercises of the forenoon were about the same as the day before. The boys all felt that their learning was to be of the most practical kind, such as would help them in the business of life. All education does this, but all boys cannot realize it.

The first business of the afternoon with the second class was to put up the shelves they had made the day before. Of course, the boys had to go through a great many forms that were useless to experienced workmen.

"Now, my lads, we are to nail the shelves to the brackets," said Mr. Brookbine. "To do this correctly will be a nicer job than you have yet done;

but you must work carefully, and give strict attention to the directions. With the larger try-square draw a light line eight inches from each end of the shelf, and on the top."

"Which is the top?" asked Dick Short, as he looked on both sides of the board in the hands of Phil Gawner, who was his bench-partner.

"Either side will answer for the top, but you should take the best side — the one with no rough places in it — if there is any choice. Always put the best side out: there is no cheat in it in carpentering. It is not like putting all the poorest apples at the bottom of the barrel."

The students selected a side for the top, and ruled the lines.

"Now draw another line on the other side, seven inches and a half from the end, — a more decided line than the other. Good! Now put one of the brackets in the bench-vise, and screw it up tight. Put the wide end of the bracket up, and about two inches above the top of the bench. — Tom Ridley, you have got it four inches. — Ben, you are not more than one inch. — You must learn to measure distances with the eye. That will do.

"Here are several kegs of nails, which I opened

this forenoon. We have spikes, tenpenny, eightpenny, sixpenny, shingle, and lath nails. There are two kinds of the same length, as a tenpenny or an eightpenny board-nail, or a finish-nail. Board-nails have a broader head, and are stouter than a finish-nail. Which kind shall we use for the shelves?"

"Finish-nails," shouted half a dozen boys at a venture.

"Eightpenny finish will be about right. No. 1 will nail to the first bracket, and No. 2 to the second. No. 2 will take the board, and lay the end on the bracket, and No. 1 will nail it. Fix the shelf exactly against the mark on the under side. Hold the board very still; and, when the nailer gets it exactly right, he should put his left hand against the bracket, grasping the board at the same time."

The instructor did it himself, and all the nailers observed how he did it.

"The light line on the top is to show you where the nails are to be driven. Now go ahead. Strike so as to hit the nail squarely with the face of the hammer, so that it will not bend the nail, or slip off and mar the board."

He had to stop half of them, and give them a little outside practice with the hammer. But the boards were nailed on. They were tried with the square, and then nailed against the wall, between the windows. The planes were put upon them, and the boys were proud of their first job.

CHAPTER XXIX.

AN AFTERNOON IN THE MACHINE-SHOP.

THE first class of the Beech-Hill Industrial School were most of them older than the members of the second class. All of them had attended high-schools or academies, and made more or less progress in the studies to be pursued. But they had no better knowledge of practical mechanics and the use of tools.

Mr. Jepson, the instructor in the metal department, had served his time for seven years as a machinist in England, and had worked at his trade a great many years in America. He was competent to build a steam-engine or to run one, and had learned his trade with more thoroughness than most American mechanics.

One of his specialties was drawing; and he was to teach this branch, which is the foundation and corner-stone of all practical mechanics. In his opening speech to the class, he said that the first thing in doing a job of any kind was to make a plan or picture of whatever was to be constructed.

Unlike the carpenter, he did not begin by giving the names and uses of the various tools on his bench, and on the walls near it. He told the boys what could be done in brass, iron, and steel. He pointed out in what manner chemistry and geometry, as well as natural philosophy, if not absolutely essential, were exceedingly valuable, to the machinist.

"I don't believe half the machinists know any thing about these branches," said Bob Swanton.

"I don't believe a quarter part of them learned any thing about these sciences, or even drawing, in school; but they have had to learn them in working at their trade," replied Mr. Jepson. "In forging iron, in casting any metal, in brazing, soldering, and many other operations, one must learn the effect of heat upon metals, and the effect of various substances upon them.

"Do you think an old-fashioned blacksmith don't know some of the uses of borax? Why does the tinman use resin, or some chemical preparation, in preparing and soldering his wares? Why does the blacksmith cool one piece of iron by putting it in water, and let another piece cool off on the floor, if he don't know any thing about the science of chemistry?"

"I meant book science," added Bob Swanton.

"All science is the same, whether it be in a book or in a man's head," added the instructor. "You must get it into the head to have it of any use to you, and it matters not where it come from. All I mean to say is, that a theoretical knowledge of science, such as you get in school, will be of very great advantage to you in the mechanic arts."

"We are willing to admit that," said Lew Shoreham rather impatiently; for he was in a hurry to get hold of the tools, as the second class were.

"Here is a bar of brass, half an inch square," said the machinist, taking the piece of metal from his bench. "We can do almost any thing with it that we can with wood."

"You can't saw it, and plane it as you can a piece of wood," said Will Orwell, who had probably never been in a machine-shop in his life.

"Certainly we can: why not?" demanded the teacher.

"Saw brass!" exclaimed Will. "I never saw any such thing done."

"Did you ever see a watch made?"

"I never did; but"—

"Then, you ought to believe that a watch can't be made," interposed the machinist.

"It looks absurd to me to talk of sawing brass, and I don't believe it can be done," persisted Will.

"Possibly I may be able to convince you that it can be done: in fact, I know I can, if you are not very unreasonable," added Mr. Jepson, as he put the bar of brass into one of his iron vises, and screwed it up tight. "Now, stand by me, and see that I don't deceive you."

The machinist took a hack-saw from a hook in front of him.

"There is the brass in the vise, and here is the saw," continued the instructor. "I shall saw the brass bar into two pieces, and I shall do it about as quick as an amateur would saw a piece of hard wood of the same size."

"That thing don't look like a saw," Will objected.

The instructor took from a drawer a package of hack-saws, on which there was a label.

"What does that say, my lad?" asked Mr. Jepson, handing the package to the sceptical student.

"One dozen hack-saws," Will read on the label.

"Here is one from the package, and you will see that it is just like the one in the frame. It is a saw without a particle of doubt."

"It looks more like a file."

"It is not at all like a file."

"Dry up, Will! Admit that it is a saw, and don't argue the question all day," interposed Lew.

"I will give it up: it is a saw," added Will.

The machinist applied the saw to the brass bar, started it carefully so that it need not jump about, and then worked quite lively for a few moments. The end of the bar soon dropped on the floor, and Will picked it up.

"I grant that you have sawed brass, but I don't see how you can plane it," said Will.

"In order to plane it, I should have to put it into a planer; but I can take off shavings as long as the bar itself. I must convince you, Will, or you will never believe it."

All the boys were curious to see this operation. The bar was put into the machine, and the interested observers picked up the long and tightly curled shavings of brass. Of course, Will was convinced. Mr. Jepson then took a rod of brass an inch in diameter, and held it up before the class.

"This rod is also of brass: it is not made of cheese, though you will think it can be cut about as easily as though it were cheese," continued he, as he fixed the rod in a turning-lathe. Running on the belt with the lever in front of him, the rod began to turn with tremendous rapidity.

The boys gathered around the lathe, and the machinist took up a tool made of an old file. He applied it to the brass, and the metal shavings began to drop rapidly upon the frame of the lathe. In a few moments the end of the rod became a shining ball. The metal could hardly have given less apparent resistance if it had been cheese.

With various tools the machinist soon had a cup next to the ball. Then he made an ogee form, and a dozen other shapes, until the boys were utterly astonished at the results. It seemed incredible to them that brass could be cut as easily as soft pine.

"I suppose that can only be done with brass," said Oscar Chester.

"It can be done with iron just as well, though the operation will be slower; or with steel, and then it is still slower," replied the machinist, as he adjusted a rod of iron in the lathe.

With no more difficulty than before, though not so rapidly, he cut the same form as in brass. With another lathe, he cut a screw on an iron rod. Taking a blank nut, he put it into the vise, and applied the proper tap to it, cut the female screw, and then put it on the rod. Then he cut a screw with a stock and die on a piece of brass wire, and tapped a nut to fit it.

He went to the forge, and welded a couple of pieces of iron together, and had something to say about tempering metals. Taking an old brass candlestick, he sawed the pedestal into two pieces, which he held up before the boys, and then allowed them to examine the parts. He then brazed them together so nicely that the boys could hardly see the place where it had been sawed.

"Are we to learn to do all these things, Mr. Jepson?" asked Pemberton Millweed.

"That is what you are here for," replied the instructor. "But you will not begin with the lathe and the plane; and there is a great deal of hard work to be done at this trade."

"What is the first thing we are to learn?" inquired Bob Swanton.

"Filing."

"Filing! We can do that now!" exclaimed Lew Shoreham.

"Not one of you can do it properly. Any one thinks he can do it, but a nice piece of filing is one of the most artistic things in the trade. It cultivates the eye and the hands, and you could spend months at it without exhausting the subject. But I dare say we are not to go into the extreme niceties of the art. I can tell you this, my lads: if you should work at the trade of a machinist for fifty years, there would still be something to be learned, and greater skill to be obtained."

"Then, we are not likely to become full-fledged machinists in six months," added Pemberton Millweed.

"Certainly not, but you can learn a great deal in that time; and, if you follow the trade for a living, you will have to keep learning all the time you work at it. In America, apprentices, if there are any now, only work six months or a year, and really learn the trade, if they learn it at all, after they go to work as journeymen. Labor is too valuable in this country for a man to spend seven years in learning a trade: besides, one who has worked six months at a trade becomes valuable to his employer."

"But we are to learn a lot of trades in six months or a year," suggested Harry Franklin.

"Not at all: the only trades you are to learn are those of machinist and carpenter. Incidentally you are to learn a score of other things. When we find out what the boys are best for, we shall put them mainly to that. It is a good thing for a machinist to know something about carpentering, and for a carpenter to be able to handle a piece of iron as well as a piece of wood.

"Almost every trade now is subdivided into several. Formerly a carpenter did every thing about a house. Now the doors are made by one concern, the blinds by another, the stairs by a third, the floors are laid by a fourth, the lathing by a fifth: all the mouldings are done by machinery, and so on. So it is with many trades: they are cut up into specialties. Now, if you please, we will go to work."

On this side of the shop there were a dozen short benches, each supplied with tools, which were fewer and simpler than on the carpenters' side; for much of the work was to be done by machinery. Out in the floor were several lathes for heavy work, a planer, a boring-machine, a circular-saw for metals, a grindstone, several emery-wheels and polishers, — in fact, every thing that could be required for work in metals.

Mr. Jepson gave out several blocks of iron, and required the boys to put them in the vises. Then he explained the large number of files belonging to each bench, gave each student a drawing of the form into which he was to file his metal, and set them at work.

Passing from one pupil to another, he instructed him in the work before him. The boys soon found that they had not taken an easy job, but they did not complain. Some of them soon learned to handle the file with some degree of skill, and the instructor began to have some idea who would make machinists among them.

When the school was dismissed for the day, the pupils were directed to go on board of the Sylph.

CHAPTER XXX.

WHAT THE STUDENTS FOUND AT THOMPSON'S POINT.

AT the scholastic session, in the morning, the scholars had been forbidden to take any of the boats without special permission, which would not be granted to those who were not qualified to manage them. The Goldwing, and a sloop called the Emma, were the only sailboats belonging to Beech Hill.

Besides the two four-oar quarter-boats belonging to the Sylph, there were four other rowboats, two pulling four oars, and two pulling two oars, each. When the boys went on board of the steam-yacht, they noticed that all the rowboats were made fast to her stern. It was evident that the present excursion was for the purpose of drilling the boys in rowing and handling boats.

Captain Gildrock had been away all the afternoon, and returned only in time to join the school in the steamer. Bates had got up steam, for he had learned to be a man-of-all-work, from hoeing corn, up to steering a steamer. Dory was sent to the pilot-house, but no one heard the instructions given him. Oscar went with him; but, if Dory knew the programme, he did not speak of it.

The ship's company all went to their stations, though there was nothing for the cooks and stewards to do. Oscar steered until the steamer was near Thompson's Point, opposite Split Rock, when Dory took the wheel. The captain had instructed Thad Glovering, the first officer, to get the anchor ready. Dory ran the steamer into a bay next to the point; and, when she was within a quarter of a mile of the shore, he rang to stop her.

"Back her, Dory," said the captain, who did not wish to go too near the shore. "That will do: let go the anchor."

"Now, my lads, we are going to learn to handle boats before we sail any more," said Captain Gildrock. "It is often as important to be able to handle a boat properly, as it is to be able to sail the ship. We are rather short of instructors in the art of rowing, but we shall do as well as we can. I will take the port quarter-boat, and Dory will go in the starboard."

"The Goldwing Club know how to row," suggested Dory. "They can do all that I can, though that isn't much."

The captain admitted that they could row very well, for he had seen them do it; and he appointed the other four members of the club as coxswains of the remaining boats. In a few minutes they had all embarked, and, as directed, had assembled around the port quarter-boat, from which Captain Gildrock told them all that could be told in regard to the art of rowing.

"You will obey the orders of the coxswains without grumbling, or asking any questions," continued the captain, when he had given the pupils the names of the different parts of an oar, and shown them how to use it. He was in favor of a man-of-war stroke, especially for beginners; for it was slow and measured.

The Goldwing Club had practised it a great deal, for the skipper had learned it of his father. The boats separated, and each coxswain proceeded to tell what he knew about rowing "man-of-war fashion." Many of the boys were disposed to indulge in a little skylarking, and some of them were not inclined to obey the orders of the several members of the Goldwing Club. But the captain was too near to permit any thing like an outbreak.

But the boys were greatly interested in all aquatic sports, and in an hour's time they could pull a very fair stroke. They learned all the man-of-war boat terms, and could "toss" and "let fall" with tolerable precision.

"Pull to the end of the point," shouted Captain Gildrock, as his boat led off in that direction.

The other boats followed him. As they approached the shore, the coxswains discovered that there were several persons there; though it was generally an unfrequented spot, without a house within a mile of the point. The rowers, being back to the shore, could see nothing. The coxswains wondered what the sensation was to be, for they were satisfied that there was "something in the wind."

Even when the boats touched the beach they could see nothing, for the point was covered with trees. Captain Gildrock landed first, and the coxswains had hard work to prevent their crews from following him pell-mell. But the discipline was preserved without breaking any thing, till orders came for all to go on shore. The boats were all hauled up so that they should not get adrift, and the several crews followed the captain up the hill.

"Hurrah!" yelled those who got to the road first.

Doubtless this yell gave expression to their astonishment as well as their enthusiasm. In the road, which leads down to the end of the point, they found two long vehicles, the pairs of wheels on which were twenty feet apart.

Standing by the side of them were two men, who were the teamsters, and two boys of seventeen, very genteelly dressed. On each vehicle was a boat, each of which was hardly less than fifty feet long. They were both broad for rowboats, and were finished in the most elegant style. The students were delighted, and could hardly find words to express their enthusiasm.

"Six oars on a side! Twelve oars in one boat! Who ever heard of such a thing?" exclaimed Will Orwell.

"You would not have believed there was such a boat, to say nothing of two of them, if you had been told about it," said Dave Windsor mischievously.

"I believe in them both now," replied Will. "Do you suppose they are for us?"

"I think they must be. I don't believe there is any other concern in these parts that would have any use for such boats," added Dave.

"My lads, here are two new pupils, from the city of New York. I hope you will give them a cordial welcome, and make things pleasant for them," said the captain, interrupting the comments of the boys on the boats.

"Hurrah for the New-Yorkers!" shouted Ben Ludlow; and three lusty cheers were given in response to the captain's introduction of the new boys.

"This is Luke Bennington, and his father is a shipbuilder. He knows a ship from a cooking-stove, and can give you all points in boating. The other is Matt Randolph, whose father is captain of an ocean-steamer; and he can do any thing in a yacht except splice the main-brace."

The two boys began to bow as they were introduced, and kept it up until the principal ceased. Then they went in among the boys, and began to shake hands with them, and to make themselves acquainted.

"What about those boats, Captain Gildrock?" called Bob Swanton, after he had met the new-comers.

"Those are twelve-oar barges such as they use in the navy. They are single banked, and will accommodate nine persons in the stern-sheet," replied the captain. "They were built in New-York City especially for the Beech-Hill Industrial School. I expected to have had them a week ago, but they were not finished. Luke Bennington and Matt Randolph came up in charge of them. Now, if you are ready, we will put them into the water."

The barges were unloaded, and conveyed to the lake. As soon as they were in the water, the students gave the usual three cheers. Of course, they were not satisfied until they were seated in them; and there were now just students enough to man them, without any coxswains. They pulled off to the steamer, towing the other boats. The boys were sorry to get out of them so soon, but there was no more than time to reach the school before six o'clock.

The new boats were the subject of much enthusiastic talk that evening, but they were not to be used until four the next afternoon.

That night two more students arrived, and the complement intended was exceeded. Dory was moved into the mansion, and also Thad Glovering, so that the dormitory would accommodate them. Of the new boys it happened that three of them were qualified for the first class, while the fourth was admitted to the second class.

The next day the studies, and the work in the shop, went on as before. It was a new thing to the boys, and the captain did not expect any difficulty at present; and he had none, beyond the little bits of mischief which were not at all serious. Dory was superlatively happy in the snug harbor he had found after the wanderings and trials of the earlier part of the year.

The deep interest of the principal in the institution induced him to give his personal attention to every thing that was done. He was in the schoolroom most of the forenoon, and in the shop most of the afternoon. But his teaching was done mostly on board of the Sylph, and in the boats. When he found an opportunity to improve the minds or hearts of the boys, he used it, wherever it happened to be. His instructions were always welcome to the students.

The practice in swimming was kept up every day during the rest of the season, unless the weather was unfavorable. In a fortnight most of the boys could swim very well; but half a dozen of them had not yet obtained the confidence to strike out, without the planks, into the deep water of the lake. The two New-Yorkers were fine swimmers, and their example and suggestions were valuable to the others.

On the day after the arrival of the barges, the students gathered at the lake for the exciting exercise of rowing. They were gathered on the temporary wharf built for the accommodation of the Sylph.

"We have not got things to rights here yet, my lads," said Captain Gildrock. "I was thinking this summer of building a suitable wharf and boat-house, but I concluded to let you do it. We can have two boat-clubs now, and we want a hall for them to meet in during the winter. You are to build this house."

"Build a house!" exclaimed Bob Swanton.

"That was what I said, and what I meant," replied the captain. "It will be a boat-house, large enough for all the boats on the lower floor, and for a club-room on the second floor."

"Can we do it?" asked Ben Ludlow.

"If you can't do it, with Mr. Brookbine's assistance, I might as well discontinue this school at once. I find that boys work best, and enjoy it more, when their labor is to accomplish a result. You will not only build the house, but you will, I hope, make the plan for it. When you get a little farther along with your drawing, you will be competent to do it.

"I shall offer several prizes for the best plan, and build upon it when it is accepted. We shall also build a wharf of stone at the same time, and that will be a part of the plan. I want you to think how you would do it all as you have opportunity.

"For the present," continued the captain, "the first class will be machinists; and the second class, carpenters. I think it is better, therefore, to give one boat to the first class, and the other to the second. Each of the classes may organize a boat-club at once. I should like to have each one choose a coxswain now, before you get into the boats. Don't do as the American people often do, — select one who don't know any thing about the work he is to do. Elect one whose orders you will be willing to obey.

"This election will be of temporary coxswains. In a week or two, when you have learned more about boats, you can do it more understandingly than now."

The students were delighted with the idea, and a lot of them fell to electioneering as naturally as the average American citizen. In the first class, Matt Randolph was elected; in the second class, Dory Dornwood received very nearly a unanimous vote. The coxswains were directed to take the command at once, and they proceeded to number their men. Then they were assigned to their places. Dory was the first to get his boat off, and he led the way out into Lake Champlain.

Each coxswain exercised his crew for an hour; and, of course, they had to have a race. As Dory had all the Goldwing Club with him, his boat won it; though the boys in the first class were older and stronger than those of the second. Captain Gildrock had told them that each club might name their own boat, and every student was requested to propose a good name at the next meeting. They had a great deal of fun over this subject.

When the name of "Leader" was first suggested, it met with favor; but Ned Bellows, who had proposed "Winooski," said he would vote for "Leader" if the other boat would call their barge "Follower." The joke was carried so far that a committee was appointed to wait on the other club, and suggest the name of "Follower." Of course, the first class were indignant; as the suggestion was a reflection upon their position at the end of the first race. The names finally adopted were "Gildrock," in compliment to the captain, and "Winooski," one of the rivers of the State.

Perhaps the students enjoyed themselves more in these elegant barges than even in the Sylph. Before the season closed, they made many excursions in the Gildrock and the Winooski; and with all the practice they had, under the best instructors, they could not well avoid becoming first-class oarsmen.

As they continued their work in the shop, some of the boys developed a very decided taste for the mechanic arts; some preferred carpentering; others were fascinated with wood-turning, after the lathes were in use; not a few desired to be working machinists; and some desired to learn only enough of the latter trade to enable them to run a steam-engine to the best advantage.

After finding out what trade best suited each boy's taste and ability, the captain intended to allow him to work mainly at that trade, though not to the neglect of any other essential knowledge. To say that all the boys were delighted with their occupation, with their work in the school-room and the shop, as well as their play on land and water, would not be stating the truth too strongly. Even Pemberton Millweed was proud of his accomplishments when he could make a bolt, with a screw and nut: and it is even probable that he forgot the meaning of the word "genteel;" at any rate, he did not use it any more.

Bolingbroke became a good mechanic as well as a good scholar,— all the better mechanic for being a good scholar. Both of the farmer's boys were glad they failed to find places in stores; for they were satisfied in less than a month that they could earn more money, be quite as respectable, and more independent, as mechanics.

Elinora liked her place in the store, where she had fair wages. She paid her board at home, and was independent of everybody. The captain found plenty for Fatima to do, and she proved to be a very valuable clerk to him.

The boys look out of the corners of their eyes when they see Mr. Darlingby with her, as he is a great deal of the time when they are not about their work; and even the principal fears that he may lose his accomplished assistant in the care of the records and his correspondence.

Farmer Millweed seemed to have become a new man, as well as the new head of his family. Captain Gildrock took the mortgage on his farm, and lent him money to pay his interest and the more pressing of his other debts. His daughters pay their board, and the eight dollars a week from this source is a godsend to him.

Mrs. Millweed does not say much about the new order of things, but she cannot help seeing and appreciating the improvement in their circumstances; for the farmer is certain that he shall be able to pay all his debts in time, and own his farm free and clear.

Affairs went on very smoothly at the Beech-Hill Industrial School for several weeks, though in time the institution had its trials and troubles; and we are content to leave the " Champlain Mechanics" in their "Snug Harbor," expecting to present them again when they begin their promised work with the "Square and Compass," in the practical work of "Building the House."

www.ingramcontent.com/pod-product-compliance
Lightning Source LLC
Chambersburg PA
CBHW021151230426
43667CB00006B/351